Luck to Levens

Glimpses of a Westmorland Parish and

its Inhabitants Through Time

Luck to Levens

Glimpses of a Westmorland Parish and its Inhabitants Through Time

Stephen Read, Ian Hodkinson, Geoffrey Cook, Allan Steward and Gillian Wood

Levens Local History Group

2014

Levens Local History Group

Luck to Levens
Glimpses of a Westmorland Parish and
its Inhabitants Through Time

ISBN 978-0-9931122-0-1

Printed by

MTP Media, Kendal

2014

Contents

Credits and Acknowledgements

Many people have helped the members of Levens Local History Group in writing this introductory history of Levens. We are most grateful to those who have given freely of their time and knowledge, and have lent their personal and important documents including deeds. We especially thank the following who either loaned or donated their photographs and allowed them to be reproduced: Mr and Mrs C.H. Bagot, Mrs B. Steele, Mrs M. Moore, Mrs M. Staniforth, Mr and Mrs C. Mason, Mrs C. Hope, Mrs A. Clarke, Mrs G. Wood, Mrs M. Knipe, Mrs A. Coxon, Mr L. Walling, Mrs A. Agnew, Mrs A. Seymour, Mrs H. Caldwell, Mrs A. Halhead, Mr D. Cottam, Mrs D. Hartley, Mrs B. Fairlee, Mr and Mrs F. Martin, Mr M. Sisson, Mr M. Pond, Mr and Mrs A. Steward, Mr D. Willacy, Mrs N. Mallinson, Mr and Mrs M. Whitelock, Mrs Rosemary Benson, Mr and Mrs F. Routledge, Mr and Mrs K. Ashcroft, Mr T. Addison, Mr J. Lancaster, Mr B. Moffat, Mr J. Marsh, Mr D. Metcalf, Mrs R. Pedley, Mrs N. Geisler, Mr A. Merkel, Mrs B. Woof, Mr J. Goodland, Mr A. Hayton, Mr J. Hodgkinson, Mr J. Marsh, Mrs R. Wadey, Mrs L. Mrkalj, Mr J. Quartermaine (Oxford Archaeology North), The Trustees of Levens Methodist Chapel, The Governors of Levens Church of England School, Mrs G. Rodd, P.V. Dobson & Company Limited, Cumberland and Westmorland Antiquarian & Archaeological Society, Levens Women's Institute, Cumbria Library Services (Sylvia Kelly and Jackie Fay), Mr T. Elliott, Mr S. Read, Prof I.D. Hodkinson and especially the publishers and editor of the *Westmorland Gazette*. Hubert Simpson's photographs of peat cutting are reproduced courtesy of Miss Jean Simpson. We also thank The Museum of English Rural Life, University of Reading, for permission to use the photographs of Thelma Clarke from a *Farmer's Weekly* article published in 1946. Pictures of Sidney Swann and Prof William Stephenson are from open access sources at the United States Library of Congress and the Library of New South Wales, respectively. Images from the Domesday Book are reproduced from *Open Domesday*, a digitised copy by Prof. J.J.N. Palmer, University of Hull.

The front cover illustration is reproduced courtesy of *Sothebys* Auction House of London. The rear cover illustration of Levens Hall is from the *Lonsdale Magazine and Kendal Repository* of 1822.

We apologise if we have unknowingly infringed copyright in the use of any photographs.

Foreword

For many years I have wished to see the history of Levens village recorded and so I am delighted to have had the opportunity to be involved with the production of this book. Levens has been the home of my family for well over a hundred years. My earliest memories are all of here and I am happy that I have been able to return to once again live in the village.

The name of this South Westmorland village derives from the old English personal name, Leofa (or Leoffwine) and ness, meaning a headland. It refers to the tract of land between the rivers Kent and Gilpin that unite at the southern end of the parish where they flow out into Morecambe Bay. Elderly natives of Levens will tell you that they live 'on' Levens, rather than 'in' it – on Leofa's headland.

The present village of Levens is made up of the hamlets of Beathwaite Green, Cotes and Causeway End. It became known as Levens after the church was built, but the old name of Beathwaite Green was in common use well into the 20th century. As a small child I vividly remember being asked by an elderly gentleman where I lived and on replying 'Levens' he said 'Beathwaite Green' in a somewhat disparaging tone. In the 19th century Beathwaite Green had the reputation of being the abode of wild men and less than respectable women – a far cry from the upmarket image Levens has today!

The title of the book, *Luck to Levens,* refers to the toast that all visitors used to have to make when they visited Levens Hall which was 'Luck to Levens while t'Kent flows'. The reason for this was because in the 17th century a malevolent gypsy put a curse on the house predicting no male heirs would be born to the family living at the Hall until the river Kent ceased to flow and a white fawn was born in the park to the herd of black fallow deer. Therefore the toast was made to wish luck to the family while the river was flowing.

This book attempts to tell some of the history of Levens using old photographs, most of which have not previously been published. The pictures have been collected by Levens Local History Group over a number of years. We are very grateful to all members of the group and the wider community who have so generously contributed their pictures and their memories for use in the book. We very much hope that you will enjoy reading it.

Gillian Wood
Chair : Levens Local History Group

Chapter 1. Introduction

1.1 The southern part of Levens village at Causeway End in 1914

This is the classic view of Levens village seen by people travelling east-wards across Levens Moss, nowadays on the A590 trunk road. It shows the hamlet of Causeway End, with the spire of St John the Evangelist's church protruding above the trees to the left [see 5.7]. The view is now much changed by the construction of several new housing develop-ments at this end of the village. Nevertheless, one still gains the im-pression of Levens as comprising a cluster of light coloured houses sit-ting on a ridge overlooking the Lyth Valley to the west and the estuary of the River Kent and Morecambe Bay to the south. It demonstrates clearly that houses in those days were built well above the flood plain! The valley floor, together with other areas of the township, was part of the substantial area of common that was lost to communal use through the Heversham Inclosure Act of 1803 and the Heversham Inclosure Award of 1815. The current system for draining the valley was substan-tially created as part of that change and was supervised by Drainage Commissioners. Their obligation to maintain the rivers and main catch-water drains, together now with their associated pumps, has passed to the Environment Agency.

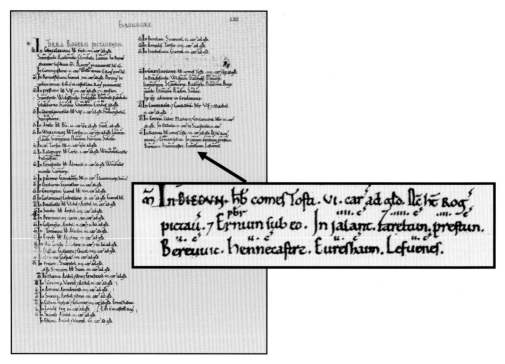

1.2 Levens in the Domesday Book

The Domesday Book, completed in 1086, is a written document that records the great survey of much of England and parts of Wales that was carried out for William I of England (William the Conqueror). Men were sent out to each shire of England to discover and record the extent and value of holdings of land and livestock by each landowner. At the time Levens is shown as belonging to the Amounderness Hundred in the Area of Westmorland in the County of Yorkshire. The enlarged section at the bottom of the right column refers to Yealand, Farleton, Preston [Patrick], Borwick, Hincaster, Heversham, and lastly Lefuenes or Levens. The taxable value of Levens, then under the tenant-in-chief Roger de Poitou, was calculated as 25 geld units. The names of people associated with Levens at this time are given as Alcolm, Almund, Arnbrandr, Arnketil, Berengar de Tosny, Bo, Clibert, Earl Tosti, Earnwine, Earnwine the priest, Erneis de Buron, Fech, Gamal, Gamal Barn, Gillemicel, Gluniairnn, Gospatric, Karli, Ketil, Machel, Machern, Orm, Roger de Poitou, Sten, Svartkollr, Thorfinnr, Uhtraed, Ulf, Ulfkil and William de Percy. The name Lefuenes is most probably of Anglo-Saxon origin meaning 'the headland habitation of Leoffwine/Leofa'. Lefuenes was originally the name of the manor associated with what is now Levens Hall. Since the establishment of the ecclesiastical parish of Levens in 1913 the name has been more widely applied, superseding the old village name of Beathwaite Green and its associated hamlets of Causeway End, Bridge End, Cotes and Sizergh Fell.

1.3 Cottages at Beathwaite Green, Levens

This undated watercolour painting by the renowned landscape artist and watercolourist Peter de Wint (1784-1849) provides our earliest visual glimpse of Levens village. The exact site of the cottages is not stated but is probably at the top of Levens Lane at its junction with Church Road looking south, where now stands '1 Church Road' and the entrance to the playing fields. A plan of 1824 shows the building and names the occupier as 'Spooner'. It was also adjacent to the old school allotment.

Peter de Wint developed an exceptionally broad and sweeping style and is regarded as one of the great masters of pure watercolour. He painted extensively in Lincolnshire, the Trent Valley, Wales and the Lake District. He came to Levens Hall several successive summers in the early 1800s to instruct the then owner, The Honourable Mary Howard [see 9.6], in the finer skills of watercolour painting. Mary Howard was normally in residence at the Hall from late July to the end of October. Further examples of de Wint's work can be seen hanging in Levens Hall [see 1.4]. This image of the Beathwaite Green watercolour, auctioned in 2000, is reproduced courtesy of Sothebys, London.

1.4 Levens Hall in 1869

This line drawing of the north elevation and entrance of Levens Hall [see 4.25] was used by Thomas Weston in 1869 to illustrate his account of *Levens Hall, Westmorland*, published in the *Archaeological Journal* 24, 97-120. The first stone-built dwelling at Levens Hall was a medieval pele tower, built by the de Redman family of Yealand Redmayne between 1350 and 1400. It was bought by Alan Bellingham of Helsington Laithes in 1562. The Bellingham family chose Levens as their main residence in the 1590s and incorporated the fortified pele tower into a gentleman's residence. Additional buildings have since been added, such as the South Wing commenced in 1692, and the Howard Tower in 1807.

Levens Hall is famous for its topiary gardens laid out and planted by Guillaume Beaumont between 1694 and 1697 [see 7.7-7.9]. The associated Levens Park is part of a much earlier medieval deer park or hunting enclosure, one of the oldest surviving examples of such parks in England. It was landscaped by Beaumont at about the same time that the gardens were being laid out, three hundred years ago. It is notable for its long avenue of oak trees that formed the original driveway to the house and for its resident population of black fallow deer and the rare breed Bagot goats.

Chapter 2. Highways and byways

2.1 Main Street, Levens around 1900

This picture of Main Street, looking north, was taken around the turn of the 20th century. The building on the right was the Post Office, run by Frederick Coward. Further up the street the white building was the Royal Oak public house. The last innkeeper was Jane McCrone, who ceased trading in 1912 when the licence was not renewed. It was noted that the proportion of people to licensed premises had fallen and that there were four licensed premises and one beerhouse within a radius of three miles. The McCrones had held the licence since 1891 but it was considered a poor house with little accommodation, whereas the Hare and Hounds, 600 yards away was a very good house [see 5.4].

The Royal Oak later became the living accommodation for the butcher's shop and the barn became the slaughterhouse. It was first run by Jack Simpson, then by Charlie and Frances Mason. Mr and Mrs Eckersley took over about 1957 and after they left Barry and Sheila Oldfield added a bakery to the butchers. It has now been made into two private residences, the single storey slaughterhouse having had an upper storey added. The small building on the left of the photo in the 18th and early 19th centuries was part of a smithy.

2.2 Main Street, Levens around 1920

Taken from the road junction, this picture shows Main Street at a slightly later date than the previous one. A horse and cart is turning into the track, alongside the post office, which led to the rear of the Royal Oak .

2.3 Main Street, Levens around 1920

This view of Main Street, looking south was taken around 1920. The two cottages in the foreground were known as 1 & 2 Langdale View and were converted into a Post Office with living accommodation in 1970 by Jimmy and Renee Prickett when they separated the Post Office from the general stores, which they sold to Gordon and Gill Rodd. All the four properties north of the Royal Oak, one of which was a lock-up shop, had belonged to Elsie Fletcher.

2.4 Main Street, Levens around 1950

Again a view looking south down Main Street but this is sometime later, probably c. 1950. The cottage in the foreground, now known as Tudor Cottage, was at one time owned by Levens Hall. Mr Robertson, Head Gardener at the Hall, lived there for many years after his retirement.

At the time of the picture the next cottage was run as a shop by Elsie Fletcher, who was blind in one eye. She is the woman in the photograph. The young man is Jackie Keast and the younger woman is possibly Dorothy Keast, his sister.

2.5 Main Street, Levens in 1972

This is a view of Main Street in about 1972, looking north. The village telephone kiosk used to be by the side of the shop. Behind Main Street, on the area now occupied by Oakwood Close, were hen huts and in the 1960s George Price, the cobbler, had a wooden hut from which he plied his trade. Before this he had his cobbler's shop at Hill Top, where he also lived.

2.6 Causeway End cottages around 1910

Causeway End cottages are situated north of the Hare and Hounds public house [see 5.4]. As their name suggests, they were built on the higher ground at the east end of the causeway across the Lyth valley, now known as the Old Road. In the 18th and 19th centuries these cottages housed mainly agricultural labourers and their families, who supplemented their income by selling peat. The growth of Kendal's population increased the demand for peat as a fuel and cottagers from Levens supplied this need. However, by the end of the 19th century the peat trade declined until in 1906 only one peat dealer, Henry Cross of Causeway End, is listed in *Bulmer's Directory*.

2.7 Causeway End from the Old Road in summer around 1914

This is a summer view of the Old Road with a hay stook on the right, covered against inclement weather. The Hare & Hounds public house's light-coloured gable end and main building [see 5.4] are clearly visible. The row of cottages to its left is on Causeway End, which was soon to become Lowgate, a main access into the village from the south. In earlier times, during the 18th and 19th centuries, when peat cutting served domestic and industrial needs, Causeway End was separated from Beathwaite Green to the north by a large common or green called the Lot. Causeway End was the area where peat cutters and agricultural labourers lived.

2.8 Carcer, Carsar or 'Causey' End, in 1899.

This view shows the Old Road (Long Causey – 'causey' being the local pro-
nounciation of 'causeway') looking east towards Levens, with St John's
church steeple on the skyline [see 5.7]. Causeway End Farm is on the right,
with the existing Hare & Hounds pub gable end just to its left. Old Road
itself was formerly an ancient packhorse route to Gilpin Bridge and on to
the Cartmel peninsula via Newton. This route was 'floated' across the
mosses on bundles of birch and heather. The 1818-20 turnpike road, with its
now demolished toll house at Gilpin Bridge [see 5.7], was of a similar construction, but lay just further south, on the approximate line of the present
A590. The two-storey building on the left, originally a peat cote, became a
single-storey cottage with a barn in which James Strickland ran a saw
bench.

2.9 Scout Scar from Causeway End around 1920

This view shows the then dirt road from Causeway End dipping down
to become the road now named Underhill, which leads from Levens
Catchwater Bridge up towards the main village centre. Old Road (Long
Causey) bears off left over the bridge. In the limestone scarp on the
right is a small cave. Scout Scar, itself outside the parish, is the impres-
sive limestone escarpment, running nearly three kilometres to the north,
forming an eastern edge to the upper Lyth Valley.

2.10 Church Road around 1910

A view south down Church Road to the properties now known as Highgate House, Highgate and Church Cottage, with St John the Evangelist church beyond [see 5.7]. Note that the road surface is made of tamped limestone without tarmac. The barns/outbuildings on the right are now incorporated into Highgate House. Only Church Cottage appears unchanged to modern eyes. That cottage's single-storey, the original Boys' School in Levens, shows it was converted from one of a row of four peat cotes or barns, the other three being formed into two dwellings.

2.11 Church Road still without tarmac around 1940

These bungalows on the north side of Church Road were built in the early to mid-1930s. At that time, Christopher Gardner Thompson, a Kendal solicitor who had bought Greengate Farm [see 4.2] in 1927, began to sell those fields that ran from behind Greengate House [see 4.1] to St John's church [see 5.7] as individual building plots. One of the first to be built was the bungalow on the left of the photograph known as 'Lockerbie', which was the home of Mr Newall, former headmaster of Levens School.

2.12 Boys playing at the bottom of Whitegate hill

This view, looking from Whitegate, is taken from its junction with Brigsteer Road, seen bottom right. The narrow roads are unsurfaced and undeveloped for housing. The field to the left, now occupied by a row of bungalows, appears less steeply sloping than the present front gardens. The first building on the left was recently used for the Post Office but is now a residential property, Langdale View [see 6.18]. There is also a clear view of the gable end of the Methodist Chapel [see 5.12] that is now partly obscured by a hedge. The boys in the picture are playing at hoop rolling, in which the hoop is rolled along the road controlled by a wooden stick.

2.13 Bungalows on Jackson's Lane around 1960

A view looking towards Whitegate hill. Note the telegraph poles and the tree in the field on the left that have now gone. The old police house and the district nurse's house are just off picture to the near right but the notice board in their garden stands just behind the wall.

2.14 View down Hutton Lane in about 1926

This photograph, taken looking north down Hutton Lane towards Scout Scar, shows the wayside properties that border the road down to Cotes and Cinderbarrow. Earlier Ordnance Survey maps name this road as Cinderbarrow Lane and it is uncertain when the somewhat inappropriate change to Hutton Lane was introduced. On the immediate left is Larchwood Cottages, which before 1903 was known as Pear Tree Bank [see 4.12] and on the immediate right is Nicholas House [see 4.13] with a sign reading 'Chocolates and Minerals' and which later was run as a sweetshop by Miss Newby. Both buildings have now been extended on their downhill sides. The other buildings visible on the left, although partially obscured by trees, are South View and then Black Castle. On the right the wall immediately below Nicholas House belongs to Sea View Cottages [see 5.11], which are set back from the road and thus hidden. The next visible house is Grey Mists [see 4.11], followed by The Orchard, Orchard Cottage and Rockgate. The name Sea View is a bit of a misnomer as the sea is only visible in the far distance today.

2.15 Lower Hutton Lane about 1900

This photograph is taken from lower down Hutton Lane than 2.14, just below Larchwood Cottages [see 4.12]. On the left is South View, the house purchased by the Levens schoolmaster George Stabler [see 9.2] for his retirement. His family continued to live there after his death and one of his sons, Oswald Stabler [see 9.5], was a well-known, if somewhat eccentric, member of the village community up until his death in 1956. The garden served for a long time as home to the Stablers' mini-menageries and plant collections. George's children, including Oswald and Bertha, are reputed to have kept a range of wild animals as pets [see 9.4]. Nowadays a two-storey extension bridges the gap between the main house and the outbuilding alongside the road. Further down on the left is Black Castle, a name that first appears in 1840 but whose origin is unknown. To the right of the road the bicycles are leaning against the wall of the then Sea View Cottages. Below this are Grey Mists [see 4.11] to which is attached The Orchard and, below this, the four cottages that were converted in the early 1920s to form those now known as Orchard Cottage and Rockgate.

2.16 Levens Lane around 1930

In 1927 Christopher Gardner Thompson sold Greengate Farm [see 4.2] to Jane Steele, retaining a substantial area of land for development. She sold the four plots of land upon which, in the early 1930s, were constructed the properties in the photograph, and which are now known as Woodcroft, on the right in the photograph, Sunnyside, second from the right, Greenways, third from the right, and Scar View, on the left. Woodcroft was built between 1933 and 1934 for Thomas Wilkinson, who then was the grocer on Main Street, Levens. The house remained in the ownership of the Wilkinson family until late 1970. Jane had the left-hand bungalow built for herself. It was then called 'Gilthrigg', but she sold it in 1936 and later built another bungalow on her adjoining land, not in the photograph, which she also named 'Gilthrigg', hence the first property's change of name. 'Gilthrigg' was a shortening of Gilthwaiter-igg, the Steele family's former farm at Skelsmergh near Kendal.

2.17 Entrance to the Levens Hotel and Garage around 1930

Brettargh Holt [see 6.7-6.9] was operated as a hotel, the Levens Hotel, between 1920 and 1940. This picture shows the lodge and entrance way from the old A6 trunk road, the main west coast traffic artery from Preston to Glasgow and Edinburgh. It is notable that the country house hotel advertises its own garage and resident mechanic, a testimony to the wealth of their clientele in the days when private motor cars were beyond the reach of the ordinary person. The lodge can still be seen, hidden amongst the trees on the north side of the A590 dual carriageway, opposite Brettargh Holt driveway, just west of the Brettargh Holt roundabout. The hotel's owners could never persuade the local magistrates to grant a drinks licence. If a guest required, say, wine with their dinner, the porter, Mr Huntley, who wore a uniform with a frock coat, would be dispatched on his bicycle to the Strickland Arms to fulfil the order. The last hotelier, Samuel Ashcroft, went on to develop the Lyth Valley Hotel.

2.18 The Strickland Arms junction around 1937

As a main refreshment stop for travellers and local folk, the Strickland Arms [see 5.1, 5.2] has remained largely unchanged externally since its construction when the turnpike linking Kendal with Milnthorpe was improved. The new alignment by-passed Sizergh Fell Side, Frosthwaite Farm, and the adjacent Duke of York inn (now Woodside Cottages), going directly to Levens Bridge, where it met the newly built north-of-the-sands section of the Ulverston to Carnforth turnpike. The superseded stretch of road is the one we see curving round the rear of the Strickland Arms. Mr Ellison, steward for the Sizergh Castle estate, learning of the proposed realignment, had the Strickland Arms built on the site of an old quarry, thus capturing the passing trade of travellers between Milnthorpe and Kendal as well as that of those from Levens and the West.

2.19 Levens Bridge junction before and after the motorcar

The top picture shows logging wagons, laden with coppiced wood, probably destined for the bobbin mill at Crooklands, crossing south over the original Levens Bridge and the River Kent [see 3.2-3.6]. Note the stone wheel-guards along the base of the parapet in both photos. The lower picture shows the junction looking north with a beech tree growing in the triangular island in the road and the Automobile Association telephone box on the right. Village youngsters used to sit around the beech tree – girls to one side, boys the other. Just over the wall, in the park, they played a game called 'guinea-pig'. The player would say how many paces they'd make it fly, then, placing a round block of wood with a chip off the edge on a stone, would hit it, making it leap forward. Traction engines would normally use the ford in the River Kent, just beyond the tree, to draw their water.

2.20 The old A6 at Levens Hall around 1928

The lower picture shows the end of the newly made Princes Way, which was opened in 1927. The newly laid surface, pavement and walls are clearly shown. The length of road alongside the Hall wall, and Levens Bridge itself, however, proved to be a bottleneck for traffic. A public footpath was made inside the wall to the right to protect pedestrians, but traffic could not easily pass. Accordingly, around 1928, the road was converted into the dual carriageway with the trees seen on the right now growing in the central reservation, and Levens Bridge itself was further widened [see 3.6]. The old toll bar cottage on the left, which stood at the junction of Ninezergh Lane, was demolished at the same time [see 6.15]. The upper picture is taken a little further along the same length of road but with a bus travelling in the opposite direction.

Chapter 3. Shaped by water
The rivers and wet mosslands

3.1 Stepping Stones across the River Kent around 1905

This photograph shows a party relaxing in the warmth of an Edwardian summer and confirming the timeless dictum that boys cannot leave water alone, except when it comes to washing themselves. The stepping stones were situated at the old ford where Nannypie Lane crossed the river to Sedgwick. They are believed to have been washed away during the 1920s.

The suspension bridge at the gunpowder mill can be seen in the background. Gunpowder manufacture was established on the Sedgwick side of the river in 1764 by John Wakefield. A second mill was opened in 1790 at Basinghyll below Force Bridge, again on the Sedgwick side. Manufacture moved to Gatebeck in 1852 with Basinghyll continuing as an incorporating mill until 1935. A separate company opened in 1857 on the west side of the river, and, with various names, notably The New Sedgwick Gunpowder Company Limited, produced gunpowder until 1935. Its site is now that of the Low Wood Caravan Park.

3.2 Levens Bridge before widening

This view, taken looking south, shows the main road crossing the bridge, with what is now the spur onto the A590 on the right. Before the M6 motorway was built the A6 was the main western route for road traffic to Scotland from England. Its strategic significance is emphasized by the WWII pill-box, still standing overlooking the bridge, opposite Levens Hall. According to English Heritage the listed bridge probably dates from 17th century, and there is earlier evidence of a bridge here on Saxton's 1567 map of Cumberland and Westmorland. Historical records from the 18th and 19th centuries highlight the continual problem of maintaining Levens Bridge in good repair, given its vulnerability to damage by violent floods and the general wear and tear caused by passing traffic of horses and heavy wagons. The impression given is one of periods of benign neglect until serious deterioration resulted in some 'great decay', about once a decade, that demanded remedial action. Before the turnpikes, all road maintenance had been a parish responsibility, but major bridges, like Levens Bridge, had long been in the control of the county High Constable as 'bridgemaster'. In the late 19th century the new county councils took over sole responsibility before central government, currently through the Highways Agency, took responsibility for major routes.

3.3 Paddling in the Kent at Levens Bridge around 1883

The view shows young lads paddling in the Kent, downstream of the bridge. Note the extent to which ivy had been allowed to get a hold on the stonework. It is no wonder that in 1901 the County Surveyor reported that Levens Bridge parapet walls were giving way and that the spandrels needed rebuilding. It was resolved that the work must be done at an estimated cost of £20, with power to spend such further sum as the County Surveyor may find necessary.

3.4 Levens Bridge, upstream view from, around 1900

The ivy is extensive here as well. Note the boom across the river to prevent the Levens Park deer from escaping downstream.

3.5 Levens Bridge in the mid to late 1920s with buses crossing

The top picture shows a bus belonging to K Bus Company of Kendal, cross-
ing Levens Bridge on its way to Carnforth before the bridge was widened.
The lower picture shows a bus of a slightly later vintage in the livery of the
Dallam Motor Bus Company on the Kendal, Milnthorpe, Arnside route.
Based at Milnthorpe, this company, like many others at the time, owed its
origins to the ready availability of ex-army lorries sold off at the end of the
First World War and converted into charabancs by firms such as John Faw-
cett & Sons of Milnthorpe. The bus pictured, however, was made by the
Vulcan Motor Engineering Company of Southport. The pictures illustrate
how a bridge, built in the days before motorised vehicles, was having to
carry an increased load of heavier traffic.

3.6 The widening of Levens Bridge in 1931-32

The top photograph shows the south side of Levens Bridge undergoing modification. This was an important step forward, enabling the A6 to Scotland to accept two lanes of traffic, one north-bound, the other south-bound. This photograph should be compared with those of the original, narrow single-carriageway bridge [see 3.2, 3.5]. From underneath, the join in the arches is still visible. Jack Mason was the quarryman responsible for providing the parapet stones from the limestone scar just below the Hare & Hounds public house at Causeway End.

The lower photograph shows the bridge, looking south, following widening.

3.7 Old suspension footbridge in Levens Park

A view looking upstream. Eileen Steward, a Levens resident, recalls being very scared because the boys would make it sway when a girl was
on it. A footway of two narrow planks was hung beneath the twin ca-
bles that formed the 'hand-rails'. Its presence in a position where the
employee or the trespasser could get at it would be unthinkable today.
It was removed in the early 1980s.

3.8 Old Force Bridge on the River Kent around 1910

This view, from downstream, shows the old single-span Force Bridge, now demolished, over the River Kent. This bridge, was replaced by the present single-span bridge in 1968. It carries the minor road from the Brettargh Holt roundabout, across the River Kent south to Hincaster and north-east to Sedgwick and Natland.

3.9 Force Falls on the River Kent around 1910

Force Falls is situated below Force Bridge [see 3.8] on the road from the Brettargh Holt roundabout on the A590 to Sedgwick. Here the River Kent is channelled through a narrow limestone gorge where the river has cut through the horizontally shelving limestone. The rocks on which the elegantly dressed people are standing are covered when the river is in spate. The main channel visible at this point was blasted out with explosives to improve river flow for the passage of fish.

3.10 Flooding in the Lyth Valley

The lower Lyth Valley, with its main river the Gilpin, has always been susceptible to flooding. These views show the extent of flooding in 1967 (above) and 2009 (below). The earliest extant drains, the Levens Catchwater to the east, and the Crosthwaite and Lyth Catchwater to the west were established in pre-Tudor times. In the 18th century a grid of drainage channels was developed, emptying into the two main catchwaters. This system was unique, comprising of high-level drains and ditches for pasture land and a lower-level system that drained waters from former peat 'benches', utilising lower level ditches and 'soughs' (tunnels) that conducted water under river courses or other obstacles. It proved adequate for peat removal and summer grazing, but in the winter periods, most of the land became waterlogged. The first big improvement came with the Heversham Inclosure Award in 1815, which defined and named the drainage ditches, specifying their width and depth. Even so, flooding from Morecambe Bay, exacerbating heavy rainfall and run-off from the higher land, has been an ever-present threat. Records state that in 1852 'within two hours, the tide had overflowed the whole marsh between Milnthorpe and Lyth' and that in 1874, water was higher than in 1852. Serious flooding recurred in 1903, 1907, 1927, 1938, 1952 -3, 1967, 1977, and again in 2009, even though five pumping stations had been built between 1984 and 1991. This pumping system, the last installed, at Gilpin Bridge in 1991, has since mitigated some of the worst aspects of flooding.

3.11 Gilpin Bridge in 1955

The bridge, originally built with one arch in 1820, had a second arch added following Joseph Glynn's 1843 survey of the Lyth Valley, which brought in far-ranging changes to the waterways and drainage. These latter works cost £15,000, a sum collected from landowners and tenants by a local Internal Drainage Board levy. The river was straightened and new tunnels were dug under the high level system. The Levens and Lyth main ditches were linked after an agreement was reached between the Foulshaw Estate and Crosthwaite and Lyth. With the improved outlets, fields could be drained to sustain a longer grazing and cropping season. The first drains had been of the Speke type, which was a trench with a square channel at the bottom, covered with turf or slate. In the early 19th century, clay land tiles were introduced.

3.12 Site works for diverting the River Gilpin at Bridge End in 1981
These pictures shows construction work in progress on diverting the
River Gilpin at Bridge End and improving the out-flow of water from
the Lyth Valley Main Drain. This, by far the biggest improvement to the
drainage of the Lyth Valley in recent times, involved the construction of
a tunnel under the Gilpin and a new bridge under the A590. This bridge
incorporated sluice doors to prevent a rising tide from coming up the
river. The installation of pumps at Johnscales, Levens Catchwater, Pool
Bridge, Sampool and Ulpha (to give them their official names) overcame
the existing tidal interruption and allowed for a continuous 24 hour outfall. These views look towards Gilpin Bridge. It is at about this location,
according to the map in Paul Hindle's 1998 book *Roads and Tracks of the
Lake District*, that the two bronze-age 'corduroy' trackways [see 12.4],
one from Whitbarrow, the other from Meathop, could have converged
from the west to ford the River Gilpin.

3.13 Construction of the tunnel under the River Gilpin in 1981

By far the biggest improvement to the drainage of the Lyth Valley was instituted in 1981, with the construction of a tunnel under the River Gilpin. This photograph shows the scale of work for the new River Gilpin channel.

3.14 Replacement of the old Tudor tunnel under the River Gilpin in 1981

The old Tudor tunnel was situated some 250 metres north west of P.V. Dobson's garage at Gilpin Bridge. In addition to the Levens Catchwater to the east, other catchwaters, recorded as early as 1692, had already been placed along the west side of the Lyth Valley to stop run-off waters from Whitbarrow affecting the peat cutting and pasturage in the valley. However, when it was found that the best peat could be won from lower levels, it became necessary for a lower drainage system to be devised. This was to be channelled under the higher level system, using a sough (a small wooden tunnel, twelve inches square).

3.15 New Bridge Tunnel and sluice gates, Levens Main Drain in 1981

The tunnel shown is situated at Bridge End, just east of the River Gilpin. This is the site of the main pumping station capable of discharging some 11,000 gallons of drainage water per minute. Just south of this, in 1981, a new bridge was constructed to carry the A590 over the River Gilpin. This A590 bridge incorporated sluice doors to prevent the tide from coming up the river.

3.16 New embankment on the River Kent in 1924

This photograph looks upstream from close to Arnside railway viaduct and shows the outfall of the Levens Main Drain to the left being separated from the River Kent by the Brogden Bank, which was created when the viaduct was constructed in 1857. The railway company had hoped that the land thus reclaimed could be successfully farmed, but the enterprise failed through repeat flooding and the loss of the bank.

Chapter 4. From peat cote to stately home - an Englishman's Castle

4.1 Greengate House, Levens in 1899

Greengate House, on the left of the picture, is the 'ancestral' home of the Barnes family. Standing on the corner of Church Road and Levens Lane, it was initially purchased in the 1840s by James Martindale Barnes and his then wife Elizabeth as a gentleman's family residence. It was known at the time as Green Gate Cottage. It has since changed names twice: at the time of the photograph it was known as Fern Cottage, later changing to Greengate House. In the large rear garden of this house James Martindale Barnes [see 9.11], a prominent amateur botanist, maintained his living plant collections, most notably his varieties of British ferns. More photographs of the garden, together with information on James's botanical experiments are given in the garden section of this book [see 7.3-7.6]. This historic garden is unfortunately no longer there, having been recently sold for the Russell Armer housing development aptly known as Greengate Gardens.

4.2 Greengate Farm on Levens Lane in 1899

This farm, which faces south down Church Road, with the garden of Greengate House in the foreground, is of some antiquity. It is one of the early freehold farms in the parish and has a bread oven that probably is of 18th century or earlier origin. Its extensive farmland behind was sold for housing development – now Greengate Estate - the seller insisting that more than minimum space was provided between every house. The two-storey end, which had been a separate dwelling, was incorporated into the farmhouse. Here, many pins were retrieved from between the floor-boards, indicating it had probably been a village tailor's shop/home.

The name 'Greengate' probably comes from 'the farm near the gate onto the Green'. Here the drovers, after traversing the mosses on the Old Road, would come up Church Road and pasture their herds on 'the Green' whose gate was opposite the school, just south of Greengate House. They would be fed at Cook House [see 4.5] and lodged at Greengate Farm, no doubt amongst others. The original Green occupied all the land now within the triangle bounded by Church Road, Lowgate and that part of Main Street from the Lowgate junction to Church Road. It was lost as a green through enclosure following the Heversham Inclosure Act of 1803, and was divided up into a public quarry, upon which now sits St John's, and private farmland that went with Greengate Farm. [see 5.6]. It was a large tract of common land from which the present small housing estate behind the Main Street bus stop and Central Stores takes its name 'The Green'. Moreover, at this time, the relative absence of buildings made complete the separation of Beathwaite Green to the north from the cluster of pub, farms and cottages at Causeway End to the south.

4.3 Adam's Corner (Hill Lodge) around 1905

This is the house at the corner of Levens Lane and Main Street, now known as Hill Lodge, that is directly opposite Central Stores [see 6.1]. The house has now been extended, the tree has disappeared and the white-painted property is now surrounded by a high wall. The name Adam's Corner has fallen into disuse, and appears to relate to a former 19th century occupant, Adam Forsyth, a village joiner, who lived here in 1881 when the house was called Sycamore Cottage. In 1891 the house is named The Lodge, and in 1911 it is occupied by Thomas Sisson, another joiner. It is possible that the photograph shows Mrs Sisson and her three eldest daughters, Isabel, Marion and Jenny.

4.4 West View on Church Road around 1925

The earliest record for this house is in the 1881 census and it has been suggested that it is a mid-19th century barn conversion. Together with Deerholme and Grove Cottage, it was previously part of the buildings owned by James Spicer of Cook House [see 4.5]. By 1891 and through to 1911 it was occupied by two sisters, Mary and Dora Atkinson, who were laundresses. Mary died in 1928 aged 75. Later it was occupied by Lt. Col. Tomlinson, a coal merchant and 1940 British Expeditionary Force veteran. Interestingly, there were bee boles set into the garden wall.

4.5 Cook House on Church Road around 1900

Cook House is one of the oldest properties in Levens, It is situated on the edge of what once was the extensive Beathwaite Green common that, prior to the 1805 Heversham Inclosure Act, extended from the front door of the house, across the valley to the River Gilpin. Immediately outside the house was the village green where pack-horse trains would overnight, and, reputedly, buy their food and fodder from the owner of the house. The earliest current reference to the house is a deed of 1777 when John Turner mortgaged the property to Anthony Garnett. In 1849 the owner became James Spicer, a Waterloo veteran, whose family continued their ownership or occupation of a property that at times was subdivided into three households, until 1921,when Anne Beetham Spicer died. Indeed, she is likely to be one of the people in our photograph together with her companion Sarah Ann Todd. James Spicer's daughter, Jane Lamb Spicer, led an adventurous life. She died in the St Louis Poor House in 1905 where she was known as Mrs Cooper, and where she claimed that a Mr Adams had cheated her out of her savings. She had previously been married to Edward Bare, whose family kept the Royal Oak beer house [see 2.1], and Henry Hewett, who was publican of the Hare and Hounds [see 5.4], and whom she left to live with another publican in Barrow-in-Furness before emigrating to the United States of America.

4.6 Underhill around 1905

Underhill, on Lowgate, Levens, is perhaps the oldest remaining cottage in the village. It is a grade II listed building, detailed in the Historic Monuments Commission's 1934 report upon Westmorland, and has been a classic cross passage house. There are signs of the position of the old timber frame house prior to the construction of the present stone house, which was perhaps built about 1650.

4.7 Moss Edge Cottage around 1910

Moss Edge is situated on the Levens Main Catchwater adjacent to P.V. Dobson's agricultural machinery works. This photograph shows Moss Edge with another cottage adjoining. That cottage was demolished before 1965, following a fire, and had previously been used as the first Levens Reading Room, preceding the creation of Levens Village Institute [see 5.17, 5.18]. The photograph shows Mrs Marion Butterfield, her horse Jet and her cart, which she used to carry people to and from Milnthorpe and Heversham stations.

4.8 Cotes around 1950

This image shows the two old cottages next to Benson Hall, but the people have not been identified. Cotes, that area of Levens close by Cinderbarrow Farm, is likely to be so named as it used to be an area of buildings constructed for the storage of dried peats won from the mosses in the valley below, such buildings being known as 'peatcotes'. There are still some of these small, barn-like structures to be seen in the hamlet.

4.9 Quaggs Farm, Hutton Lane in August 1922

Situated on the corner of Hutton Lane and the road to Lord's Plain farm, this old farmhouse, also known as Waggs, was often occupied jointly with the now demolished Bridge House farm that stood in the middle of the valley. Nowadays Quaggs is a residential property with a ceramic workshop and art studio run by Nigel and Libby Edmondson respectively. Mr and Mrs Norman Mason, here standing outside the main entrance, were the tenant farmers in 1922. In 1912, the tenant of both Quaggs and Bridge House farms was George Mason & Sons, the annual rent was £75, and the owner was Charles Walker of Brettargh Holt.

4.10 Crag Foot on Hutton Lane in 1960

Crag Foot lies on the western side of Hutton Lane and has changed little since 1960 save a larger front porch has been added and the attached building at the side has been rebuilt. The cottage of today was converted from two cottages between 1889 and 1901. Those cottages were built on land allotted to William Addison, a basket maker, under the Heversham Inclosure Award, but which were owned and occupied by members of the Pennie/Penny family, variously agricultural labourers, carters and mole-catchers, and their tenants. The village pinfold was also allotted to William Addison and was probably where Pinfold Cottage now stands, being formerly part of the garden and orchard for Crag Foot.

4.11 Grey Mists on Hutton Lane in 1953

Grey Mists is another property that has undergone subtle changes over the years. At the time of the photograph it was run as a guest house by the owner Mrs Booth. Since this photograph was taken a front porch and doorway have been added and the facing end windows have been split to accommodate two floors internally. More recently the outhouse visible at the rear of the building has been developed and attached to a new rectangular single storey accommodation wing built in the back garden.

4.12 Larchwood Cottages on Hutton Lane in 1905

Larchwood Cottages, on the left of the picture, were formed from one small farmstead and its adjoining barn that was built by George Gibson upon land awarded to him under the Heversham Inclosure Award of 1815. The stone arched entrance to the barn can still be made out in the furthest cottage. The row of cottages was previously known as Pear Tree Bank, taking their name from the pear tree in the left foreground, which was still there in the 1960s. They are listed as such on the 1851 census and were still called by that name in 1903. The cottage now known as 2 Larchwood Cottages was originally the barn and shippon and was probably converted in the early 1900s.

Pear Tree Bank was sold by John Gibson and others to W.H. Crewdson Esq. on 12 May 1903. Mr Crewdson was the owner of Beathwaite House [see 6.2] and the cottages remained part of that estate until the late 1960s, providing accommodation for the estate staff. At one time the district nurse lived in the cottages, but from about 1945 No. 2 was always occupied by a succession of gardeners who worked at Beathwaite. Peter Blacklock, a Scotsman, was there just after World War II. He was followed by Mr White, Mr Brooks, Mr Winton and finally Mr Rummens, who remained a tenant of the Bush family long after Beathwaite House was sold to the Lancashire River Authority.

4.13 Nicholas House and Old Chapel Lane about 1910

This view shows Nicholas House situated opposite Larchwood Cottages [see 4.12], in the angle between Hutton Lane and Old Chapel Lane. Nicholas House, originally a barn, was converted into a cottage by Mrs Crewdson of Beathwaite House [see 6.2] in 1925. In the mid-20th century it was owned by Miss Elizabeth Newby who made and sold sweets and chocolates, and for a time, bread and cakes. She also sold bottles of pop and it was common to see children at her door with empty bottles, collecting three old pence for each one.

Old Chapel Lane runs behind Nicholas House. It is so called because the first Levens Methodist chapel was here, further along on the right [see 5.11]. Built about 1795 it was the oldest Methodist building in South Lakeland.

4.14 Walnut Tree House and Walnut Tree Cottage in 1943

This view shows Walnut Tree House and Walnut Tree Cottage, which are hidden away behind the Levens Institute [see 5.18, 19], the back of which is seen on the left hand side of the photograph. This view was taken looking down the unadopted lane towards Hutton Lane, with Walnut Tree Cottage and House the first and second building on the right respectively. The gateway to The Coach House, then the garages for Beathwaite House, is just visible beyond Walnut Tree House. An extension has now been added to the side of Walnut Tree Cottage facing the camera. The building on the far side of Hutton Lane is Beathwaite House [see 6.2], which was demolished to make way for the new development at Beathwaite Gardens.

Until 1837, Walnut Tree House and Beathwaite House, along with Holly Bank, Holly Bank Cottage, Scar Bank Cottage, and most of the cottages and land within the circle of roads running from the Institute crossroads down Hutton Lane to Cinderbarrow Farm, then uphill to the Crossings and so back to the Institute, formed the Scar Bank Estate, belonging to Abraham Garnett. Over the years Walnut Tree House functioned as a farmstead and tannery, with its tannery pits at the rear of the property, whilst Walnut Tree was a smallholding with a barn in front (now Levens Village Institute) which doubled as a hammer shaft manufactory. The Gibson family [see 4.12] owned Walnut Tree and its barn, and the Claughton family [see 4.16] were the last to operate the tannery, an adjunct of their butcher's business, at Walnut Tree House.

4.15 Smithy House and Cottage (Levens Smithy) at the cross-roads in the early 1950s

This picture was taken looking up Lowgate towards the Levens cross-roads, with Smithy Cottage and Smithy House (what is now Gateside Cottage) on the right. Up until the mid-1950s there was a working smithy in the outbuilding alongside Gateside Cottage. The last black-smith was Joe Fletcher who in 1939 had succeeded his father Joseph within the business. Joe also owned the smithy at Bridge End [see 6.11] which he continued working up until his death in 1969. More recently Gateside Cottage and outbuilding provided accommodation for Levens dairy run by David Knipe. The house now known as Fletchers' Corner stands in the former smithy garden.

Smithy House and Cottage were built in 1842 and owned by Mathew Brockbank who lived at Bridge End. In 1851 Alexander Kirkbride was the blacksmith at Levens while William Brockbank worked Bridge End smithy. Joseph Fletcher Snr came to Levens in the 1890s as an apprentice blacksmith to George Brockbank, from whom in 1928 he bought Smithy House, Smithy Cottage and Bridge End Smithy.

4.16 Birks in 1908

Birks, the property that lies to the south of the A590 dual carriageway, is built upon land that was awarded to the Addison family under the terms of the Heversham Inclosure Award of 1815. It remained in the ownership of various members of that family until 1887 when it was sold to Thomas Claughton, who was a butcher in both Levens and Milnthorpe, and who lived at Walnut Tree House [see 4.14]. In 1937 it was sold to the Clarke family and in 1948 to the Wilson family, within whose ownership it currently remains - a remarkable 200 year history with only four family owners.

4.17 Bridge End cottages around 1900

This view, taken from the south-east, shows the row of three cottages built on the north-side of the old turnpike road in about 1818. The one nearest the camera and the middle one are now derelict. A second row of cottages was built to the east up to the junction with the Causeway Road (approximately where P.V. Dobson's garage now stands) with the end cottage of that row being the tollhouse for the turnpike [see 6.12].

4.18 Heaves Farm in 1946

This picture shows Thelma Clarke [see 9.15], the post lady with her post bike, making a delivery at Heaves Farm. The farm, which is part of Levens Hall Estate, is situated on an elevated position to the northeast of the village centre, on the back road from Levens to Sizergh hamlet. The Wilson family owned the farm from the 16th century. Henry Wilson, the first Alderman of Kendal in 1575/6, was described as a member of the Wilson family long settled at 'Heaves in Helston'. The earliest documented reference to the farm is of 3 August 1635 when Edward Preston of Greenyat, Beathwaite Green let the property to Henry Chamber of Sedgwick. The initials of William Wilson and his wife Ann, daughter of Richard Diccanson of Beetham, and the date 1665, are carved on a traditional spice cupboard in the kitchen of the farm. The Wilsons lost the Heaves estate, including Heaves Farm, through the indebtedness of Richard Wilson, whose creditors sold the whole estate to the Gandy family in 1832. There is a deep cellar under the parlour. Here a fatal accident occurred in 1834 when Nicholas Holme, a young servant carrying a barrel down the steps, slipped and fell, with the barrel landing on his chest. In 1946 the article about Thelma's post round described the scene with these words, 'where everything looked as though it had been there, just like that for several hundred years'.

4.19 Whinthwaite House around 1960

Whinthwaite House, on Brigsteer Road is now a private dwelling but in the 1960s it was used as a guesthouse. The house was built in 1874 for David Henry Fenton, the manager of the Kendal branch of the Lancaster Bank, on land originally awarded to Trinity College, Cambridge, under the Heversham Inclosure Award of 1815. The land and gardens that went with the house extended throughout the triangle of land between Brigsteer Road, Sizergh Fell Road and Whitegate, and also included the fields on the opposite side of Brigsteer Road. On Mr Fenton's death in 1896, all this estate was bought by Colonel Herbert Wilson, a well-known Lancaster solicitor, who donated a portion of the grounds to Levens Women's Institute to enable them to construct their hut [see 6.6]. The proprietors of the guesthouse were Jack and Clara Wilkinson, who also ran an egg production business from the buildings on the other side of Brigsteer Road. When they sold in 1965, the grounds were divided up for development, and the house was bought by Barbara Harrison, who was a generous benefactor of Levens Village Institute.

4.20 Hyning in 1906, just after a fire in the stable block

The earliest reference is of 1645 when Thomas Nelson of 'the hyninge' sold some land to Sir John Preston. Hyning has a date stone of 1853, with the initials F J G, which records when the original cottage was extended into a gentleman's residence. F J G stands for Lieutenant Colonel Frederick Gandy and Jane Gandy. He was born in 1812 the second son of J.P. Brandreth, and married Jane, the heiress of James Gandy of Heaves [see 5.5], in 1846, changing his name by Royal Licence in 1859. The 1910 Land Tax survey records that the property remained in the ownership of the Gandy family, and that the tenant was Mrs E.M. Benson, who had been there since 1891. The main house is described as, 'Stone built, walls rough-casted, slate roof, in fair repair. Built 1853. Contains small hall, drawing room, dining room, study, morning room, butler's pantry, lamp room, kitchen, scullery, larder, back kitchen, 3 cellars & coal cellar, 1st floor 4 main bedrooms, linen closet, bath room & w.c., 5 other bed rooms, small veranda to south front. Stables – coach house, 3 stall stable, barn over (used for concert room), drag cart shed, cast iron roof. Potting shed & loose box. 2 wooden store rooms. 3 loose boxes, wash house, harness room, stick house. Water, now from Lupton supply, laid on 2 years'. Emily Margaret Benson, then a widow, was the daughter of Rev. George Frederick Weston, Vicar of Crosby Ravensworth and Mary Wakefield, daughter of John Wakefield, of Sedgwick House. Emily's husband, Constantine Benson, born in Milnthorpe, was a successful American banker, a forefather of Kleinwort Benson. Emily lived at Hyning with her daughter, Mary, and they, together with Annie Gandy from Heaves, Agnes Argles from Eversley and Louisa Walker from Brettargh Holt, served on the committee of the Kendal branch of the National Union of Women's Suffrage Societies between 1908 and 1918.

4.21 Sizergh Fellside Farm in the 1920s

Above the farmhouse porch is a date stone of 1734 with the initials RIH and two carved birds. The stone was possibly put there at the time of the marriage of Richard Harrison and his first wife. He remarried in 1764 to Eleanor Mattison of Hayfellside, Kendal. He died in 1789 leaving the property to his son Richard Mattison Harrison. Richard attempted to sell the farm by auction in 1806, when it was known that the new turnpike road would divide the farmhouse from most of its land, but was unsuccessful, although it was later bought by the Stricklands of Sizergh. It still forms part of the National Trust's Sizergh estate. It was originally a small farmstead and is a relatively late example of a fire-beam house and retains many original features. Its plan consists of a 17th century firehouse with parlour and pantry. Later a staircase and kitchen were added to the east and in the 19th century a room with a cellar below was added on the north side.

At the time of this photograph Sizergh Fellside was farmed by W.O. Kitching who was there from 1916 until his death in 1944. It is now let as a private house.

4.22 Levens Brow around 1920

Levens Brow, part of the Levens Hall Estate, is adjacent to Lawrence House Farm on the old A6 road, near Levens Hall. At this time, the house was rented by Mr and Mrs Robert Bush, who eventually bought Beathwaite House [see 6.2]. They are probably the people in the photograph.

4.23 The Gardener's cottage at Levens Hall in 1915

The head gardener lived in this cottage from where he had an oversight, in more sense than one, of the topiary and surrounding gardens. The cottage was built for the first gardener Guillaume Beaumont c.1690 [see 1.4] and has been occupied by every head gardener since. Remarkably they have numbered just ten in the succeeding 324 years.

4.24 Gamekeepers Cottages, Levens Hall Estate around 1900

This photograph shows the Levens Estate gamekeeper's cottages with one of the keepers, Mr Isaac Hall [see 9.16]. The cottages are situated at the northern end of Levens Park on the east side of the river and face into Levens Park. The main access, however, is by a rear entrance that abuts onto the Sedgwick to Hincaster road. It is not known when the cottages were built but they feature on the Levens Hall Estate map of 1816. These cottages are presumably where John Michie [see 9.1], son of the Levens gamekeeper and later to become the King's Factor on the Balmoral Estate, spent part of his early childhood.

The eccentric cross-dressing Cumbrian artist Percy Kelly also spent a short part of his colourful life, from May to November 1971, in the right hand cottage. Kelly had fallen on hard times and through the generosity of Robin Bagot he was offered a short term tenancy on the cottage at a low rent. While in Levens he wrote a series of *Letters from Levens* to Norman Nicholson the Cumbrian poet, the texts of which were published in David Cross's book *Cumbrian Brothers* in 2007. These letters are typical of the many letters he sent throughout his lifetime to friends and acquaintances, which, since his death, have been recognised as important works of art in their own right. The text of the written letters is often ornately illustrated with coloured paintings or drawings in Kelly's unique style. For more on Percy Kelly see
 http://www.levenshistory.co.uk/people/Percy%20Kelly.pdf

4.25 Levens Hall over the ages

So much has been written about the history of Levens Hall [see 1.4], home of the Bagot family, there is little point in repeating it here. Readers seeking more information should look at the Levens Hall website (http://www.levenshall.co.uk/) or read the official guidebook.

4.26 Force Cottages around 1909

Force Cottages, part of the Levens Hall Estate, are situated just above Force Falls and south of Force Bridge [see 3.8] that carries the minor road from Brettargh Holt roundabout over the River Kent to Sedgwick. The cottages were built about 1690 and improved in the 1820s. Those tenants who were not estate workers or agricultural labourers were likely to be employed at the adjacent Force Mills, or Force Forge, which was situated on the right bank of the river just below the cottages, or one of the several gunpowder works in the vicinity [see 3.1]. Nearby stone walls contain evidence of the water-powered foundry and hammer-forge in the form of highly magnetic lumps of iron slag.

The cottage in the foreground of the top picture, at the time of the photograph, was occupied by Mrs Alice Grindal [née Hayton], who can be seen with her daughter Lena Hayton and William, Thomas and Molly Grindal. Her husband, John Grindal, worked as a carrier at the gunpowder works. He died in 1912.

4.27 Nether Levens around 1910

The Dallam Estate has owned Nether Levens, also known as Low Levens, since 1694. The house has a date stone of 1594, at which time it belonged to the Preston family, but references to it go back into the 13th century. As with Levens Hall, which was previously known as Over Levens, it is an early medieval fortified site. The huge kitchen wing chimneys are prominent in these images, which date from the early 20th century when the Cottam family were the tenant farmers.

4.28 Sizergh Castle

The Sizergh Estate was given to The National Trust in 1950 by the then owners, the Hornyold-Strickland family, making the Trust one of the largest landowners in Levens parish (1600 acres). The original lands, owned by the Deincourt family from the 1170s onwards, passed into the Strickland family in 1239, when Elizabeth Deincourt married William de Stirkeland. In 1336 Sir Walter Strickland was granted permission by Edward III to enclose land as his exclusive park, used for rearing and hunting deer and which extended from Brigsteer Woods to Larkrigg. The main core of the 'castle' building, illustrated above as rear and front views, is a solar tower associated with a surrounding Tudor manor house. Subsequent modifications included extension in the Elizabethan era and additions to the Great Hall around 1770. The Strickland family were prominent Royalists and Catholics and went into voluntary exile in 1688 at the court of James II in France. Walter Strickland was given permission to return eleven years later, an impoverished Jacobite, but by the mid-18th century, the family was able to restore its fortunes, largely through the careful management of the estate in their absence, by their stewards, Thomas Shepherd and William Ellison. Notable within the surrounding grounds is the limestone rock garden, constructed by T.R. Hayes of Ambleside in 1926, and the fern specimens that now form part of the National Fern Collection.

Chapter 5. Vice, virtue and victuals
Important public buildings

5.1 The Strickland Arms in the 1950s, when the A6 was at its door.

The Strickland Arms Inn [see 2.18, 5.2] was constructed for the Stricklands of Sizergh Castle in or about 1840 as an investment property by the famous Kendal architect George Webster. William Ellison, the steward of the Sizergh estate, took advantage of a change in the local road system with the re-alignment of a turnpike road, completed in about 1825. The old road is that which now runs steeply up behind the inn, passing the front of Woodside Cottages, which was then the Duke of York Inn, before running down to Levens Bridge. The new turnpike cut the corner, missing out the Duke of York, along the line of what became the A6 road. Ellison recognised that as fewer people now passed the door of the Duke of York a great advantage accrued to the newly built hostelry, and within 10 years the Duke of York had ceased to trade. Later, in the 1970s, the Strickland Arms almost suffered a similar fate to the Duke of York when the creation of the new Kendal bypass, and the re-aligning of its junction with the A6, meant a substantial decrease in the amount of traffic passing its door. The buildings were described in 1845 as 'new and spacious, a capital brewhouse, stable – gig house. The attics as well as the ground floor are well supplied with piped water from a spring. Also near the inn is a well accustomed smithy [se 6.10] and cottage.'

5.2 The Strickland Arms around 1960

In this earlier photograph cattle mask the main entrance to the Strickland Arms [see 2.18, 5.1]. During its chequered history the inn has had many publicans as shown below. This list is, however, incomplete as from at least 1896 the inn was leased to Whitwell Marks, the Kendal brewery, who put their own managers into the inn and whose names are not all recorded. Nor, at present, is it known exactly when that lease came to an end, so there may be several other publicans to add to this list.

1841- 1845	Roger Cummings
1849	Richard Parks
1849 - 1851	William Stainton
1851 - 52	Michael Hutchinson
1858	Enoch Brindson/Brinsden
1861-1888	George Wilkin(s)
1888-1896	James Bailey
1905-1929	John Willacy
1934	Thomas Bell
1935-1953	James W. Ibbe(o)tson
1963	Fred Kirkham Ellis
1965	Robert L. Crockford
? - 1990	Brian Stewart Blood and Jane Blood
? -1995	Peter Muschamp and Gillian Ann Muschamp
? – 1999	Alistair Keith Binnie
2000 to date	Martin Ainscough

5..3 Locals outside the Hare & Hounds public house in the 1890s

The upper view shows 'Ted Lancaster, Jim Wrathall, Thomas Claughton, Jack Prickett and ? Nicholson' in the Lowgate courtyard. Their individual identities are unknown. To the left is the stable and cart shed. Wrathall farmed Lord's Plain, Claughton was a butcher and farmed Birks, but there were two John Pricketts; one farmed Heaves, the other, Bridge End. A William Nicholson was a stockman, but for whom is not known. No Edward Lancaster appears on the 1901 census for Levens. The woman, and the man on the right, are perhaps James Atkinson, publican, and his wife Dinah.

5.4 The Hare & Hounds in 1910

The lower picture shows Annie Yapp, with one of her daughters. The boy is probably her son, John Winder Yapp [see 5.16]. Her husband, Ernest Yapp was publican from 1906 until 1933 and was probably the second tenant of Whitwell Marks, the Kendal brewery, who bought the inn from the Gibson family on the death of Annie Gibson, aged 100, in 1902. The first Whitwell tenant was John Bennett, and the third was John Cottam [see 11.1], who was publican until 1961 when he was succeeded by his widow. The layout of the inn is largely due to James Stephenson, publican from 1973 to 1989, who converted the former beer cellar into the Cellar Bar and added the porch which encloses the Lounge and Cellar Bar entrances.

5.5 Heaves in 1881 and possibly in the 1950s

Heaves Hotel, as it is known today, stands in its own grounds where the road over Duke Hill leaves the A590. The *Westmorland Gazette* of 18 June 1881 described a 'Fashionable Wedding at Heversham', at which Annis Gandy, daughter of Lieutenant-Colonel Gandy, of Heaves, married John Formby, son of the Rev. Lonsdale Formby, of Formby, Lancashire. The report states that 'In the ground adjoining the mansion was erected a triumphal arch twined with flowers and evergreens, and bearing the motto, on a crimson background, 'Long life and happiness.' (upper photograph). Matthew Hyde, in Pevsner's *The Buildings of England; Cumbria* (2010), comments that Webster of Kendal remodelled Heaves in about 1818 for James Gandy, and that the mansard roof, added in 1932 by Austin & Paley of Lancaster, is 'not an improvement'. The lower photograph, which shows the additional mansard floor, therefore post-dates that era, and may be as late as the 1950s.

5.6. Levens Parish Church and cottages on Church Road around 1920

Levens Parish Church [see 5.7-5.10] is situated at the southern end of the village on a south-west facing hillside overlooking the southern end of the Lyth Valley and the Kent estuary, with extensive panoramic views from the graveyard across Morecambe Bay. This view, taken looking down an unpaved Church Road, shows Levens Church set in its own grounds with a row of cottages similarly set back from the road.

The church was originally built by The Honourable Mary Howard [see 9.6] as a Chapel of Ease, dedicated to St John the Evangelist, in the hamlet of Beathwaite Green in the then parish of Heversham. She endowed the living with a stipend of £200 a year, £10 per annum for the Clerk and a further £10 p.a. for repairs to the church. The churchyard was added in 1913 during the tenure of Sidney Swann as vicar [see 9.14], when St John's Chapel became the parish church of Levens, independent from the parish of Heversham.

The cottages, which are still standing, now bear the names of Church Cottage, Highgate and Highgate House. Of these three, Church Cottage, immediately above the church, served for a short while (from 1823 to 1825) as the Boys' School.

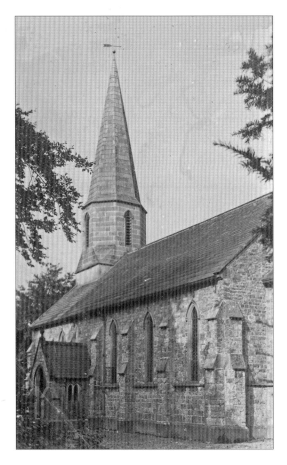

5.7. The church of St John the Evangelist, Levens in 1910

The foundation stone of St John's was laid on 7 July 1826 and the church, built of local stone, and with bricks probably from the brick-works at Heversham, was completed at a cost of £2000 on 6 August 1828. It opened for worship in December of the same year under its first vicar William Stephens. It is thought that the tower was added in 1831. The benefactor who financed all construction work was the Honourable Mary Howard [see 9.6] of Levens Hall. The architect was almost certain-ly William Coulthart of Lancaster, with the design for some of internal details such as fittings and furnishings provided by the renowned Lon-don architect Edward Blore, of Buckingham Palace fame. A vestry and small porch were added in 1873 and, in 1883 the church organ, by Wil-kinson's of Kendal, was installed. Around 1913 the Reverend Sidney Swann [see 9.14] made several minor modifications to the internal lay-out and structure and added a lych-gate and a set of bells hung on a wooden framework adjacent to the church [see 5.9]. Later alterations include a new East memorial window in 1921-22 and panelling to the chancel in 1956.

5.8 The interior of St John's Church before and after renovation in 1913

The upper view, probably taken before 1912, shows the relatively plain interior of the church before the renovations that were carried out by the Rev. Sidney Swann in 1913. This picture should be viewed alongside the similar one below taken three years after the renovation .

The Rev. Sidney Swann [see 9.14] was responsible for a number of internal changes within Levens Church in 1913. Several of these are visible in the lower photograph taken in 1916. They include a lowering and shifting of the pulpit to the right, the corbelling and decoration of the chancel arch and the ornate decoration around the east window behind the altar. In addition there are new choir stalls and clergy desks, and an organ chamber has been created. This new organ chamber, shielded by a curtain, is to the left in front of the chancel arch. At the time of renovation additional supporting beams were added to the roof.

5.9 The bells at St John's Church, Levens.

The bells, which have no clappers but can be struck manually by a hammer, are hung in a separate open structure at ground level, as the church tower was not strong enough to support their weight. Here they are shown in their original position in their pagoda-like housing. They were installed in 1912 by the Rev. Sidney Swann [see 9.14] who wrote somewhat cynically in his memoirs that 'I got three Milnthorpe steel bells which were only used for flowerpots as their tone was so evil. These I hung in a Japanese shed in the churchyard and struck with a wooden mallet that greatly improved their tone.' The Japanese styling owes much to Sidney Swann's time as a missionary in Japan between 1890 and 1897.

5.10 Levens War Memorial

The memorial was unveiled and dedicated by the Bishop of Carlisle on 4 April 1921. Major Watson-Gandy of Heaves, chaired the committee that commissioned the memorial, which was paid for by subscription. The 11ft high structure, of native limestone, stands near to the churchyard entrance. Its builder is not known. The WWI fallen are named on a bronze plate let into the stone near the middle of the cross. The names of the fallen from WWII are inscribed on a bronze plate that was designed by J.W. Howie & Sons of Kendal.

5.11 The old Methodist Chapel on Old Chapel Lane, Levens

The old chapel building is the ivy clad two-storey structure in the background. Old Chapel Lane [see 4.13], which runs in front of it, is hidden behind the wall. Since the new Methodist chapel was opened in 1892 this venerable old building has served several purposes. Initially it was used as residential accommodation but was then run by Alan Newby Stainton and his wife Bertha, as a commercial garage. Mr and Mrs Stainton were also linked with Exchange Garage, in Kendal. Mr Stainton's mother was the sister of Miss Newby who lived in nearby Nicholas House [see 2.14] and who gifted Bluebell Cottage on Old Chapel Lane to Mr and Mrs Stainton in 1962. The building was converted to residential accommodation in 1983, with additional entrances and windows added on both storeys. This interesting view, taken from below on Hutton Lane, is now largely obscured owing to the construction of the house on Hutton Lane named Sea View in 1961. The two peat cotes in front of the chapel were demolished before Sea View was built. There has been a Wesleyan Methodist congregation in Levens since the early 1790s and this old chapel came into being in 1795 when Mr John Addison gifted a house already under construction for religious use.

5.12 The new Methodist Chapel, Levens around 1910

The new Wesleyan chapel is the building to the left of the road. The completion of this building owes much to the energy of the Barnes family. James Martindale Barnes [see 9.11] was initially instrumental in reviving Methodism in Levens, as recorded in a letter, dated 1849, from the local Methodist preacher John Stubbs to his son in America. In it he mentions an 'affresh opening of the Chapel at Beathwaite Green' (Levens). James's own son, Joseph Anthony Barnes [see 9.12] then started, in 1888, an ambitious scheme to build a new chapel, which culminated in a grand opening on 17 July 1892 with both morning and evening services. A commemorative stone in the present chapel wall records the event. In his diary Joseph mentions 'what a beautiful little place the new chapel is'. Unfortunately James Martindale Barnes died in 1890 and did not live to see the opening.

The other buildings in the photograph are Levens Institute (centre) [see 5,18, 5.19] and Smithy Cottage (right) [see 4.15]. Note also that the raised ground alongside the chapel garden wall is now cut back to widen the road and provide parking spaces.

5.13 Levens School on Church Road around 1910 and the emblematic sycamore tree

This photograph shows the southern rear aspect of the school, which commanded an open view over fields to Morecambe Bay. A prominent sycamore tree (inset) stood in the front of the school on Church Road, just by the school gate. It was felled in 1993 as it had become unsafe, and the school held a ceremony to mark the occasion. The tree can also be seen towering over the school in the main photograph. This tree still figures as part of Levens School insignia. The school has educated the children of Levens for over 100 years [see 8.9-8.15].

5.14 Levens Post Office about 1910

This old photograph, probably dated at the start of the 20th century, appears to show the Post Office in the building that is now Tudor Cottage, on Main Street. Levens Post Office has been located in at least four different properties. At one time it was at Lane Foot and in the early 20th century it was at the southern end of Main Street and, latterly, at the north end of the street, in the property now known as Langdale View [see also 2.1, 2.2, 5.14, 6.18, 9.15].

5.15 Shop on Main Street decorated for the Royal Wedding in 1981

Decorated for the Royal Wedding of H.R.H. Prince Charles to Lady Diana Spencer in 1981, the shop on Main Street [see 2.5] was given the title of Best Mace Shop. At that time Gordon and Gill Rodd were the proprietors.

5.16 Winder Yapp's cycle shop at Bridge End around 1935

John Winder Yapp, the owner of the cycle shop pictured above, was born in 1900 the only son of Ernest Albert Leon Yapp and Annie Yapp née Winder. His parents ran the Hare & Hounds Inn in Levens [see 5.4] . In 1916 he was entered in the British Postal Service Appointment Book as a wireless operator, but no place of work is recorded. On 9 March and 25 May 1918, respectively, he was the wireless operator on the ship *Pyrrhus* sailing from London via Plymouth, firstly to New Orleans and secondly to New York. The crew list states he was 18 years old, stood 5ft 8inches, and weighed 10 st 7 lbs with no 'physical marks or peculiarities'. He founded Bridge End Garage in 1921 selling and repairing bicycles, R.O.P. petrol (Russian Oil Products) and repairing motor car punctures. In 1931 he married Catherine Leah Barnsley and in the same year purchased 3 cottages at Bridge Row from Peter Addison for £135. He is recorded in the 1934 *Kelly's Directory of Engineering, Hardware and Motor Trades* at Bridge End, Levens. About 1941 he sold his garage and cottages to Walter Garner. At some time he also ran a café and sweet shop from the property which is now the Gilpin Bridge Inn. He died in the Wigton, Cumbria registration district in March 1970 aged 69.

5.17 Levens Institute around 1905

Levens Institute, an old converted Westmorland barn, is the building on the left side of the photograph. In keeping with its origin as a bank barn, the main front entrance, on the uphill side of the building, is through into the main upper storey room. The rear downhill side entrance is through into the lower storey rooms. Before conversion the building had been used as a workshop. The 'new' Institute, initially known as the Coronation Institute in honour of the coronation of Edward VII, was inaugurated in 1903 and has served as a social meeting place for village functions ever since. It was initially designed as a Reading and Recreation room with a small committee room. The downstairs room housed a snooker table. A new toilet block, porch and main entrance have been added to the right of the frontage. The end of Walnut Tree Cottage [see 4.14] can be seen peeping beyond the right hand end of the building. At the time of writing there is much debate as to whether the Institute should be refurbished or whether it should be replaced by a new Village Hall built on the present village recycling area on Lowgate. An earlier Levens Men's Reading Room, which the Institute superseded, was situated next door to Moss Edge Cottage on the narrow lane that ran down the south side of Apple Tree Cottage, below South View, to the mossland [see 4.7].

The building opposite the Institute, with the cartwheels outside, is the old Levens Smithy, with Smithy House (now Gateside) and Smithy Cottage on the corner [see 4.15].

5.18 Levens Institute around 1910

Another early view of the front of The Institute [see 5.12, 5.17] on the corner of Hutton Lane, with the carved and painted sign over the doorway. The window to the left of the façade has been replaced by the double emergency exit doors. A small two-storey extension now occupies the position of the porch of Smithy Cottage on the right. Beathwaite House [see 6.12], now demolished, is visible through the trees to the left of Hutton Lane.

Formally opened on 19 December 1903, the new Institute cost £77 to acquire the former hammer-shaft workshop from John Gibson, and a further £242 17s 7d to alter it for its new purpose. Robert Newall, the school headmaster and Honorary Secretary of the old Institute, was a driving force in its establishment. He continued as its Honorary Secretary until he retired in 1945. Initially, it was a 'members only' establishment, with an annual subscription of 2/6d. Membership was limited to residents of the parish who were over 15 years of age, and judged by the committee to be 'sober and industrious and of good character'.

Chapter 6.   In Memoriam
The lost buildings of Levens

6.1 Grey Stones on Levens Lane, with the Old Levens Vicarage behind, around 1940

This view is taken from outside Central Stores looking down and across Levens Lane.   Things have changed considerably since those days. Grey Stones is the house with the dormer window standing in its walled garden with tall trees.   This house was constructed by Mr W. Head, a coal merchant, of concrete blocks containing a high proportion of coal dust and did not stand the test of time.   It was demolished and two new properties, Greystones East and Greystones West, were constructed in its place.   A similar fate befell the old Levens Vicarage [see 6.3] which is seen to the right, immediately behind Grey Stones. The porchway on the left belongs to the property known as Hill Lodge [4.3], around which a high stone wall has since been erected.

6.2 Beathwaite House around 1938

Beathwaite House, now demolished, was sited, together with its gardens, where the Beathwaite Gardens, Whitbarrow View and Nethercroft developments now stand. The estate also included the properties now known as Holly Bank, Holly Bank Cottage, Madeline and The Coach House. A substantial portion of its extensive gardens can still be seen [see 7.1, 7.2]. The original house, built by Abraham Garnett on land awarded to him under the Heversham Inclosure Award of 1815, has also been known as Scar Bank House, New Walnut Tree House and Walnut Tree House. In 1859 it was described in the *Westmorland Gazette* as being, 'of modern structure replete with every convenience for the reception of a Gentleman's Family. Contains on the Ground Floor – Entrance Hall, Dining and Drawing Rooms, Parlour, Kitchen, Larder, Pantry, Baking and Wash-houses, Brewery, Pumphouse with a never failing supply of pure spring water, large Stone Cistern, Boilers, Ovens, Ranges, Baking Plate, Etc. On the Second Floor – Two Front Bedrooms and Dressing Room, Two Back Bedrooms, Closets and Cupboards; Four Servants Bedrooms and Attics over the whole. Excellent Wine and Beer Cellars, and suitable Out-offices; Stable, Coach-house and Harness Room; Garden-house and Workshop; Large Kitchen Garden, Productive Orchard, Shrubbery, and Flower Garden and about One acre of Ornamental Pleasure Ground' [see 7.1, 7.2]. It was extended in 1908 when it was also one of the first houses in the district to be lit by gas having its own acetylene gas plant. From the 1890s to 1967 the property was owned first by the Crewdson family and then by the Bush family, both of whom were great benefactors to the parish. In 1967 the house was and sold to the Lancashire River Authority (which later became the National Rivers Authority and then the Environment Agency), to become their regional office. The offices and land were sold for development in 1993, when the building was demolished.

6.3 Levens Vicarage in 1906 (upper) and around 1910 (lower)

Levens vicarage, at first a parsonage, was built about the same time as the Church, between 1826-28, and was similarly commissioned by Mary Howard of Levens Hall [see 9.6] to be built upon land she bought for the purpose. It has been thought that the architect was Webster of Kendal, but it is now known to be William Coulthart of Lancaster, a stonemason and architect, who worked closely with the Websters.

The Vicarage was described in a 1945 surveyor's report for the Diocese of Carlisle as 'An old Vicarage house, garages and stable block, situated in garden, also a field adjoining, in all about two acres'. The surveyor commented that the Vicarage 'had [probably] originally been two cottages, and was converted over 100 years ago.' The Vicarage gardens were used extensively for the benefit of the village, providing the venue for many fund raising garden parties and events [see 10.9, 10.10].

6.4 The old Levens Boys' School before demolition in 1983

Boys and girls attended separate schools until they were merged on the current site in 1907 [see 5.13]. The old building pictured was demolished around 1983 to build the houses on Church Close. The school was purpose-built by Mary Howard [see 9.6] and her husband around 1825. School inspectors frequently found the school lacking in basic resources and with inadequate sanitation, despite the best attention of schoolmasters such as George Stabler [see 9.2]. Balancing the books frequently depended on donations from the Howard family. Soon after it ceased to be a school, the building became a weekend/holiday home named 'The Bungalow'.

6.5 The old School Master's House in 2010

The old School House stood in its own grounds next to Levens School on Church Road [see 5.13]. It was demolished in 2013 to make way for a new property, which was to provide a village home for Hal and Susie Bagot following their retirement from their stewardship of Levens Hall. George Stabler [see 9.2], the Victorian village schoolmaster and botanist, lived in this house for many years. This winter view, taken from the field below the house, shows the south-facing elevation.

6.6 The Women's Institute hut on Brigsteer Road

Levens Women's Institute was formed on 29 November 1917. The first meeting was held in Hyning Barn [see 4.20] at the home of Mrs Gandy, the first president. Subsequent meetings were held either in Levens Men's Institute or Hyning Barn. In March 1922 the secretary sent for details of a hut advertised in Home and Country. Later an advert was put in the Westmorland Gazette inviting 'tenders for a W.I. hut 100 feet by 30 feet.' In May members were officially informed of the kindness of Col. and Mrs Wilson of Whinthwaite [see 4.19] who gave a piece of land for the erection of the new building. Tenders were received and the hut constructed. The official opening by Sir James and Lady Reynolds, who were then living at Levens Hall, was on 20 April 1923. The building was spacious, had a good dance floor and was used successfully for meetings, socials, concerts and dancing until 1961. The expense of repairs and running costs was by then becoming prohibitive and it was decided to sell the hut and land. The hut, or W.I. Hall as it was then called, was eventually sold to P.V. Dobson, but the land remains in the ownership of the W.I..

6.7 Brettargh Holt when the Levens Hotel, about 1930

This building, now re-named 'The Villa', is to become once again a country house hotel. Set in its own extensive grounds [see 6.8, 6.9, 11.14], the building has undergone several transformations during its lifetime. It has also given the name Brettargh Holt to the nearby roundabout on the A590. At the time of the photograph it was operating as a stylish venue called the Levens Hotel. The land upon which the dwelling named Brettargh Holt was built was part of a larger holding that also included Park Head and Frosthwaite estates. The house we see today was built for George Henry Brettargh Yeates during 1872-73 and the architect is believed to have been Joseph Bintley, who also built Heversham Grammar School. In 1888 Brettargh Holt was acquired by Charles Walker who, in 1895, served as High Sherriff of Westmorland. The estate was auctioned in 1920 following Charles's death, and ceased to be a family home. It was bought by E. & A. Nelson, builders of Kendal, who in 1921 sold it to John A.F. Young of Lancaster, who ran it as the Levens Hotel. In 1936 Young sold it to Samuel Ashcroft who eventually sold to the trustees of the Sacred Heart Convent in 1944. Two years later, staffed by the Sisters of the Sacred Heart of Jesus and Mary, it opened as a maternity home for up to 35 single mothers. Admissions ceased in June 1968. About 1971 it was acquired by trustees on behalf of the Salesian Sisters and operated as a novitiate centre for 15 years before becoming a retreat centre for young people and groups. From 2002 it operated as 'The Time Out Project', where disadvantaged individuals and groups came for personal, social and spiritual development.

6.8 Grounds of the Levens Hotel around 1930

The Levens Hotel [see 6.7] occupied Brettargh Holt and its extensive grounds. This photograph shows the driveway from Force Lane and the well-appointed tennis courts. A flock of free range turkeys is wandering across the foreground. It seems that the hotel guests were well-supplied with festive birds.

6.9 Levens Hotel Drawing Room around 1930

The elegant refurbishment of the drawing room at Levens Hotel [see 6.7] is well displayed in this photograph. Under the proprietorship of Mr J.A.F. Young the building had undergone significant alteration in 1928, to the designs of the Kendal architect Malcolm G. Shaw.

6.10 The old joiner's shop at Sizergh

This building, situated opposite the side garden at the Strickland Arms public house [see 2.18, 5.1, 5.2], started life as a smithy around 1840, and its tenancy was usually linked to that of the Strickland Arms. In 1851 the licensee of the pub was William Stainton and on the census he was listed as being a blacksmith and victualler. By 1905 John Willacy was the licensee. He added the timber extension to the stone building and it was by now a joinery business. In the 1930s it was taken over by William Latham who had been employed by Willacy's. He retired in 1950 and sold the business to Arthur Fletcher who had worked for him and who had served his time with Willacy's. Arthur Fletcher had the business until 1978 when he sold up and retired. After this, the building, which belongs to the Sizergh Estate, was only used for storage and fell into disrepair, the timber building being demolished around 2006. Over the years much of the work carried on by the joiners was related to the farm trade, cart wheels, carts, trailers and farm gates all being made. Arthur Fletcher was the last joiner in the area to make peat sluffs (spades). Joinery work required by the Sizergh Estate was also important to the business. W. Latham and A. Fletcher were also undertakers and painters and decorators for the local area.

6.11 Bridge End Smithy at Gilpin Bridge

The old smithy at Gilpin Bridge was demolished after the death of the last blacksmith, Peter Fletcher, in 2001. He was the third generation of the family to be there. His father, Joe Fletcher, the twin brother of Arthur Fletcher [see 6.10], was the previous blacksmith until his death in 1969 and he ran the smithy at Bridge End simultaneously with the smithy in Levens village [see 4.15], as did his father before him. In 1928 Joseph Fletcher senior purchased the Bridge End smithy from George Brockbank who was born at Bridge End in 1839, the son of William Brockbank. On the 1851 census the family were living at Bridge End and William's occupation was given as blacksmith. In 1906 George retired to Pool Bank where he died in 1931. During his time as a blacksmith he was renowned for making scythes. Much of the work carried out at the smithy was for local farmers, making and repairing farm implements, shoeing horses and hooping cart wheels. They also supplied Levens Hall with shears for trimming the topiary [see 7.7-7.9].

6.12 The ruins of the old Toll House at Bridge End in 1956

The old toll house stood at the junction of the Levens Bridge to Greenodd turnpike road (which was built between 1818 and 1820) with the extension of the old causeway road that ran from Causeway End crossing the River Gilpin a few hundred yards upstream of the current Gilpin Bridge at Bridge End. The site of the toll house is now part of P. V. Dobson's garage car park. It was also the most easterly cottage in the ten cottages that formed Bridge Row [see 4.17]. The survey for the 1910 Land Tax, carried out in November 1913, described the properties as, 'Old cottages stone built & slated, first five rather better than second lot. Roofs fair. No 4 being done up & soon ready for occupation. Others empty, windows boarded up. Each cottage contains front room, pantry & 2 bedrooms. Lean to sheds at back, windows of back rooms open into sheds. Range of loose boxes, stables &c at back, partly ruinous, lofts over. 3 closets at end recently repaired. Tollbar house empty.' The toll collectors who were named in the census were Thomas Schollick 1841, James Wood 1851, and James Cross 1871. The building ceased to be used as a toll house when the turnpike trusts were taken over by the local authority in the early 1880s.

6.13 The Levens Welcome, probably in the mid 1920s

Levens Welcome [see 6.14] was situated on the east side of what is now the A6, just south of Levens Bridge and opposite Levens Hall entrance [see 2.20]. It was demolished when Levens Bridge was widened in 1933. Little is now known about The Welcome. In some respects it served as the Levens Village Institute does today, although as it was a fair way from the village it was probably intended rather more for the use of Levens Estate workers. Reports in the Westmorland Gazette of the time chronicle a variety of events taking place there [see 10.2]. For example, a dancing class held in the Welcome during the winter and spring of 1920 concluded on Friday 4 June with an exhibition before a large audience of parents and others. At an exhibition held a week previously, Mr Richard Bagot received a hearty vote of thanks, and replied that he hoped this was the first of many pleasant evenings to be spent in The Welcome. Other recorded social events include a children's concert competition following the annual Levens Horticultural Society bulb show. It involved pupils from the schools at Crosscrake, Helsington, Heversham, Milnthorpe, Levens, Lyth and Witherslack competing for 40 prizes. Levens won the 'Argles' challenge shield. Whist drives in support of such diverse organizations as the Conservatives and the Levens Horticultural Society also took place in 1912 and 1924 respectively. It was where soldiers were recruited for World War I.

6.14 The Levens Welcome around 1930

These two additional views show, in the upper picture, The Welcome standing on the right, alongside the unwidened A6. The wall of Levens Hall gardens [see 2.20, 7.7, 7.8] is to the left: Levens Bridge is in the distance. A circular plaque on the end wall of The Welcome gives the mileage from Levens Bridge to Milnthorpe and London, together with a a plea for 'Safety First'. A signpost to the right indicates a public footpath. The lower picture is a view of The Welcome from behind, with the stable block of Levens Hall visible on the far side of the road.

6.15 Levens Toll House around 1926

The Levens toll house was situated at the southern end of the gardens at Levens Hall [see 2.20, 7.7, 7.8], just south of the junction of the A6 and the Ninezergh Lane. Built about 1800, by the time of this photograph it had ceased to be a functioning toll gate. In 1851 it was lived in by Thomas Benson whose occupation was given as toll gate keeper. In the early years of the 20th century the occupant was Mrs Eliza Latham who used to sell sweets on the premises. She was the mother of William Latham who was a joiner at Sizergh. On Sunday evenings villagers often used to congregate on nearby Levens Bridge to watch the world drive by, a practice now discontinued. The cottage was demolished in 1928 when the road was widened.

6.16 The old Automobile Association box at Levens Bridge in 1928

The Box was situated by the side of the old A6 road, immediately opposite the junction with the old A590 at Leven Bridge [see 2.19]. Members
of the Automobile Association were each issued with a key to the box,
which contained an emergency telephone for their use in the event of a
vehicle break down. The AA patrol man, resplendent in his khaki uniform, long leather boots and peaked cap, was part of a countrywide network of motorcycle patrols that came to the assistance of members in
difficulties. They would salute any vehicle sporting an AA members'
badge. The AA adopted its distinctive yellow corporate colour in honour of its first president, the Earl of Lonsdale (The Yellow Earl), a visitor
to Levens Hall. [see 8.25].

6.17 The old bus shelter on Levens Lane around 1970

The photograph shows the first bus shelter in Levens. Buses came through the village from the early 1920s, but no shelter was built until 1966, buses pulling up at the roadside adjacent to the village shop. Following demands from villagers, in February 1966, Westmorland County Council granted Levens Parish Council permission to construct a shelter on land belonging to South Westmorland Rural District Council, provided that the layby to allow buses to pull up to the shelter had been constructed first. The design was by John Ashworth, an architect who then lived at Scar Bank Cottage, Levens, and the shelter was constructed by Alan Hutchinson of Levens. At the same time a shelter was constructed opposite Levens Hall where a slate roof was provided and fixed, free of charge, by the Levens Hall Estate. The village bus shelter shown was replaced as part of the Queen's 2002 Golden Jubilee celebrations by the existing shelter, built by D.W. Parsons to a design by Derek Hicks and Thew, architects of Kendal.

6.18 Levens Post Office in 2009

This photograph shows the building on Main Street that was the village Post Office from 1971, when Jimmy Prickett was postmaster, until its closure in 2010. Ken and Edna Ashcroft [see 8.6] bought it in 1982 and were the last to run it. It is now a private house called Langdale View. [see also 2.1, 2.2, 5.14, 9.15].

6.19 Washdays past — washing drying on a hedge, around 1899

The picture shows washing left on a hedge and wall to dry in the sun. The site appears to be the old orchard at The Nook Farm, opposite the Hare and Hounds public house [see 5.4]. At the time of this picture a lane, then known as 'Well Road', now long overgrown, passed alongside the wall to the well that supplied the hamlet of Causeway End with drinking water.

Chapter 7. Havens of tranquillity
The gardens of Levens

7.1 Garden terraces at Beathwaite House, around 1925-30

The top picture shows the construction of the terracing below the main house [see 6.2], with infilling taking place behind a retaining wall. The spirally curved object near the centre of the picture appears to be a roll of turf ready for laying. It sits on top of what seems to be a mound of rectangular turf pieces. The plank provides easy access for a wheelbarrow. The lower picture, taken about five years later, shows the formal lawned terrace garden below Beathwaite House, with its extensive views westwards over the Lyth Valley and northwards to Scout Scar. The identity of the man tending the flower beds is unknown. This part of the garden still survives below the parking area for the new Beathwaite Gardens housing development.

7.2 Beathwaite House gardens around 1930

The footpath in the upper photograph led down from the end of the ter-raced garden at Beathwaite [see 7.1], through the small gateway shown and into the field beyond. Part of the field was fenced off and planted with daffodils and young trees in the 1950s, enhancing the view from the terrace. Whitbarrow and the Lyth valley can be seen in the distance.

The building, lower left, was known as the 'Atco' House as this was where the lawnmowers were kept. *Atco* was a brand of lawnmower. The building also contained slatted wooden shelving that was used to store apples. The formal garden, lower right, with extensive flower beds and a large pergola, was known as the 'East Garden'. The trees in the background are the ones behind the wall at the Institute crossroads. The garden now has houses built upon it.

7.3 The Barnes' family garden at Greengate House in the late 1890s

The large garden illustrated in these two photographs was situated behind what is now Greengate House [see 4.1]. This extensive garden area
was where James Martindale Barnes [see 9.11] conducted his botanical
experiments and maintained his collections of plants. The rear of Greengate House is visible in the right hand picture. Note the extensive beds
of ferns, the group of plants in which James specialised and in which he
became a recognised authority. Many eminent botanists visited the garden to admire his fern collections. In an article in the *Gardener's Magazine* of 11th September 1897, p. 563, the fern expert C.T. Druery provided an effusive appreciation of the garden, describing it as a 'Fern Para-
dise'. The person sitting in the deckchair in the left hand photograph
appears to be Joseph Anthony Barnes [see 9.12].

7.4 Fruit trees, flowers and other produce in the garden of Greengate House in the late 1890s.

Before he developed his passion for ferns James Martindale Barnes's [see 9.11] botanical interest passed through several phases. They included, among others, the cultivation of varieties of showy plants including dahlias, polyanthus and roses. He also experimented with the intensive cultivation of fruit trees under glass or in a pyramid growth form, as described by Thomas Rivers of Sawbridge, Hertfordshire in his books *The Orchard House* (1851) and *The Miniature Fruit Garden* (1858). In this picture we see fruit trees growing as cordons and espaliers along the northern wall of Greengate House garden [see 4.1]. The large walnut tree in the far corner of the garden is still there today, having survived when the garden was redeveloped for housing. In arable areas of the garden, such as the one shown, James conducted a series of experiments over 23 years to try to discover how to minimize the losses of potato crops to a disease known as Late Potato Blight. At the time this disease was responsible for the widespread 'potato famine', particularly throughout Ireland and parts of Scotland. He submitted an essay describing his results to a competition run by the Royal Horticultural Society and he won first prize. The essay was subsequently published in the *Gardener's Chronicle* pp. 439-440 and 471-472 (1874).

7.5 Fern Frames in the garden of Greengate House in the late 1890s.

These are the glass-topped frames in which James Martindale Barnes [see 9.11] reared the varieties of British fern species that he collected from the woodlands, hillsides and crags of the southern Lake District. Barnes was interested in the wide variation in the shape of the leaf or frond that was found in the British fern species and during his lifetime he discovered or named 221 varieties covering 19 fern species. He also conducted experiments to discover whether several of the more interesting varieties he collected bred true to type and whether they could be easily propagated.

7.6 The Barnes family at work in the garden at Greengate House in 1899

This picture shows the Barnes family hard at work cutting and clearing the long grass in the orchard part of the garden at Fern Cottage [see 4.1], as it was then known. The man wielding the scythe appears to be James Martindale Barnes junior, the wheelbarrow pusher is Joseph Anthony Barnes [see 9.12] and the older lady with the grass rake is most likely to be their mother, Mary Ann Barnes, the widow of James M. Barnes senior. The identity of the younger and more smartly dressed lady with a hat, who appears to be knitting, is unknown but could possibly be James and Josephs' sister, Annie Jane. Note also the ferns interspersed among the trees.

7.7 Topiary Garden at Levens Hall

Levens Hall gardens [see 1.4, 4.25, 7.9] are internationally famous for their topiary as shown above. Many of the individual trees shown can still be seen today. The upper picture is thought to date from the late 1890s, the lower from the early 1900s. The tall cedar tree in the lower photograph was blown down in the gales of January 2005.

7.8 More Topiary at Levens Hall around 1900

The upper photograph from the 1890s shows, in the foreground, two topiary pieces known as the chair and the piano. The coronation arch and the castellated yew hedge are visible in the distance. A closer view of the arch, dating from the early 1900s is shown below. The following picture shows the hedge in greater detail.

7.9 Clipping the topiary in Levens Hall garden in 1930

The topiary garden is highly labour intensive and the individual trees and hedges require annual clipping to maintain their shape. The picture shows John Elliot (right) and a fellow gardener working on the castellated hedge, with its pair of arched windows. Because of the height of the hedges and trees much of the work was traditionally carried out on raised trestles, as shown in the picture. Typically the larger topiary trees and hedges were evergreen Yew, noted for its longevity and most of the lower hedges were evergreen Box, a species also noted for its persistence. However, owing to the ravages of box blight, some low hedges have been replaced by Japanese Holly. The topiary gardens form just a part of the more extensive gardens associated with Levens Hall, which include among others, lawned gardens, wall borders, a fountain garden, a bowling green, a beech circle and hedges, a herb garden and a nuttery with vegetable borders. A full description of the gardens, including historical accounts, can be found in Chris Crowder's splendidly illustrated book *The Gardens at Levens* (London, 2005) and Annette Bagot's historical (1689-1710) account of the garden's formation in *Garden History*, 3, 66 -78.

7.10 The Avenue of oaks in Levens Park around 1900

These two photographs provide contrasting views in summer and winter. The Avenue, planted primarily with oak trees, stretches in a straight line for over 1km on the east bank of the River Kent. The exact dates of these photographs are uncertain but they were probably around the beginning of the 20th century. The identities of the gentleman (above) and the servant girl (below) are unknown. A group of the park's black fallow deer are crossing the path in the lower photograph

Chapter 8. Dressed for the occasion
Levens folk at work and play

8.1 Spectators at a ploughing competition in the Lyth Valley in 1896

Ploughing competitions [see 11.13] were a common feature of rural life. The first local competition appears to have been organised by Kendal Agricultural Society in 1810 and most local societies organised their own events, which often attracted an appreciative audience. The flat lands of the Lyth Valley provided an ideal testing ground for would-be champion ploughmen. The audience featured in the photograph appear distinctly overdressed by today's standards where wax jackets and wellington boots would be the norm. The ladies in particular are all smartly dressed in long coats over long dresses, with each displaying a fashionable hat. One lady to the right of middle on the front row appears to be sporting a fur coat. The men are similarly dressed in their 'Sunday best'. It would be interesting to know whether the refreshments were for the spectators or the ploughmen. It looks as though the metal jugs might contain a little more than a pint of good ale.

8.2 Levens Methodists on an outing in Levens Park around 1900
This photograph is taken looking from the north along The Avenue of oak trees [see 7.10] south of the gamekeeper's lodge.

8.3 The Sunday School outside the Methodist Chapel in 1942
Names given on the photograph are from left to right at back; Mrs Richardson, teacher, Nan Tolley, Audrey Tolley, Audrey Bowes [evacuee], Harold Akrigg, Richard Withers [in glasses], John Akrigg; middle; Pat Powley, Winn Newby, May Newby; front; unknown, Ruth Gibson [partly obscured], unknown, Jack Keast, Marjorie Garnett [in bonnet], Ronnie Gibson, Cliff Gibson, Ruth Newby, Derek Hartley and Pam Gibson. [see also 5.12]

8.4 Domestic staff at the old vicarage in Levens in 1928

The building in the background of the picture is the old vicarage [see 6.3]. The girls are sitting on the lawn in front of the house. The ones wearing aprons were employed as maids, the others just visiting. The vicar at the time of this picture in 1928 was the Rev. W. Bannerman.

From left to right are Mabel Kitching, Lucy Kitching, unknown, Hope Cheeseman and possibly Daisy Cheeseman.

8.5 The proud owner of a motor car outside Beathwaite House , probably in the late 1920s

This photograph, taken outside the front entrance of Beathwaite House [see 6.2], shows an 'unknown' lady standing alongside a splendid example of a Morris Cowley or Oxford motor car, built between 1919 and 1926. Note the metal AA membership badge mounted centrally just in front of the windscreen. The AU number plate indicates a Nottingham registration.

8.6 Edna and Ken Ashcroft, proprietors of the last Levens sub-Post Office in 2010

Levens has had a Post Office since at least 1851. The last Levens sub-Post Office closed in 2010. It was located in the three-storey building at the northern end of Main Street which has now been turned into private accommodation renamed Langdale View [see 6.18]. The closure reflected the national trend, with 25,000 post offices in the 1960s, declining to 19,000 in 2000 and 11,500 in 2010. Levens Post Office proved more resilient than those in neighbouring villages, whose customers often used to travel in to Levens for PO services, to pay their bills, collect benefits, tax their car and buy stamps.

This support for the local community has now been replaced by a Post-Office out-service three afternoons a week in the Methodist Chapel meeting room, coinciding with a 'coffee-shop' in the Chapel itself.

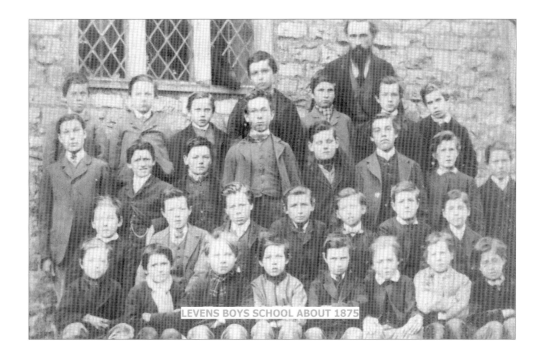

LEVENS BOYS SCHOOL ABOUT 1875

8.7 An early Levens Boys' School photograph, probably from around 1875

The first school photograph recorded in the Levens Boys' School [see 6.8] log-book was taken in 1869. Although it is now impossible to identify any of the pupils, the location is definitely the grounds of the Boys' School, and the bearded man is George Stabler [see 9.2], who came to the school as the Master, aged 21 in January 1861, with his 19 year-old sister Hannah as his housekeeper. George was the Schoolmaster at the Boys' School for the rest of his working life until failing eyesight compelled him to relinquish his post at the end of 1899. This picture dates from the early years of school photos, which were often taken by itinerant photographers. However, it looks less than impromptu, with the boys presenting themselves in their best clothing, none more so than the serious looking youth on the left. Note also the young man ostentatiously showing off a pocket watch, probably his father's. The possession of a silver pocket watch was one of the milestones of early manhood, and by the second half of the 19th century the availability of cheap mass-produced American watches made such display accessible to many.

8.8 Levens Boys' School photograph from the early 1900s

The background suggests that this image was taken in the road outside the Boys' School [see 6.4] before 1907, when all Levens schools merged on the site currently in use. This had housed the Girls and Infants since the mid 1820s. The headmaster, Robert Newall, stands on the left, looking relatively young. He came to Levens School to assist the ailing George Stabler [see 9.2] in 1895 and was Head from 1900 until he retired in 1931.

8.9 Levens school children around 1909

This picture of Levens schoolchildren [see 5.13] shows that all the children are wearing clogs and most of the girls are wearing white aprons. The tall girl in the centre of the front row is Margaret Fletcher and to the right of her is her sister, Annie Fletcher.

8.10 School dinner time, possibly around 1907

This photograph appears to commemorate something other than the usual pattern of daily life in the school [see 5.13] with boys and girls eating in the presence of three ladies. The cook Mrs Clark, is on the right, with apron and spoon as well as a dress hat. The smartly dressed lady on the far left is believed to be Theodosia Bagot [see 9.7], who regularly visited the school, of which the Bagot family were patrons. The one looking on, waving a large knife is perhaps one of the school managers or Mrs Smith the vicar's wife. Note also the paraffin lamps hanging from the ceiling: it was not until 1932 that mains electricity reached the school.

In the dinner hour, many children walked home for a meal while those from the further reaches of the parish brought food with them. The School log-book for the year November 1907/08 records that 'penny dinners' of hot soup and bread started to be provided in the newly merged school. It noted that a shed was erected and fitted up with a boiler and oil stove and in it the meals were prepared, adding that, during the winter, 160 of the above penny dinners were served per week. A further comment for the final day of the 1911/12 year revealed that dinners 'had been appreciated by a certain number of scholars, but there are still a few from a distance who continue to bring their own.'

8.11 Boys gardening at Levens School, probably around 1917

A posed group photograph showing boys tending the vegetable patch at
Levens School [see 5.13] in around 1917. Note the array of sharp forks and
different types of hoe. Would the teachers of today be happy to set their pupils loose with such a deadly set of implements? No wonder clogs and
stout boots were the order of the day. Leaning on his fork on the extreme
left is Arthur Fletcher; his twin brother Joseph Fletcher is fourth from the
left.

8.12 A later picture of boys at work in the Levens School gar-
den, probably around 1950

8.13 School PE lesson around 1938

The young woman taking this class, in Levens School boys' playground [5.13], is either a staff member of the school or possibly Miss Woodger, the then County Organiser of Physical Education. Exercise in the form of 'drill', an earlier form of Physical Education, became a part of the elementary school curriculum in the late 19th century, primarily as a response to the poor levels of fitness among army recruits. It involved various exercises performed standing in the schoolroom or yard. It was an orderly and disciplined physical activity, done in unison as prescribed by the Education Code. However, not until the early 1900s did exercise for fitness and health have a full place in education. The English Board of Education published its first official *Syllabus of Physical Exercises for Use in Public Elementary Schools* in 1904. These exercises, based on the Swedish System of Educational Exercise, used no apparatus, and became the precursor for the PE lessons shown in the photograph. The earliest mentions of Drill or PE in the Levens school log-books were 1901 and 1902, for boys and girls respectively. Sessions were taken by staff members, with County PE instructors visiting at regular intervals to supervise and monitor progress. Miss Woodger, mentioned above, was a County Instructor from 1937 to 1939.

8.14 Pupils in Levens School girls' playground in July 1964

This picture shows children playing a ball game in the playground [see 5.13]. Children were segregated between two playgrounds, one for girls and infants and one for boys, whose games were deemed too rough for the girls! The building on the right is where the school meals were prepared and on the left is the Parish Room, which was a village meeting room also used as the school dining hall. The children from left to right are: unknown, Lesley Wilkinson, unknown, Shirley Hornby, Susan James, Susan Reid, Olwen Wilson.

8.15 The Opening of the new rooms at Levens School in 1999

The extension cost £100,000 and consisted of a new classroom, office, staff room, storage space, quiet space for reading, space for special needs teaching, display area and new entrance. The PTA and the Levens School Support Group raised £25,000 towards the cost. It was opened by Mrs Mary Steele, the oldest village resident who attended Levens School, and who was presented with a bouquet. Alan Dobson, the Chair of Governors is on the left, the headmaster, Alan James, is first from the right, with John Nellist, Cumbria County Council's Director of Education on the right. The school's Community Development Centre, equipped with computers for the use of school and community, was also formally opened. [see also 5.13].

8.16 Boys' Brigade on parade at Levens Hall around 1897/98

The precise event celebrated in this photograph is unknown but it is clearly a formal parade of members of the Boys' Brigade, the organization founded in Glasgow in 1883 by William Alexander Smith. Information on the Kendal Boys' Brigade website suggests that such Whitsuntide gatherings at Levens Hall were a regular occurrence *'On Whit Monday 1897 the four Kendal Companies, with those of Endmoor and Leasgill, paraded at Levens Hall for their first Annual Inspection which was taken by Major Page Wood and Captain Bagot….. After games in the park, officers and boys were entertained by Mrs Bagot.'* The following year *'On Whit-Monday 1898. Captain and Mrs Bagot entertained eight companies of the Boys' Brigade, totalling 190 who had assembled to be inspected by Lord Henry Bentinck, and to compete for the challenge banners. Most of the companies were now equipped with dummy rifles for drill purposes.'* At this time the Boys' Brigade was akin to the local Volunteer Regiments, with military style uniforms and drill using dummy rifles. There were, however, several other linked activities, including bible classes, games and summer camps. Many Boys' Brigade officers and members joined up in the First World War and were among the numerous casualties. The War, however, altered the public perception of quasi-military organisations and the dummy riles fell into disuse. The presence of rifles in the photograph therefore suggests that it pre-dates the 1914-18 War.

8.17 Levens Brownies around 1950

This picture of the Brownies was taken about 1950 in the school playground. The Parish Room, where the Brownies used to meet, is in the background. The pack leader is Bobbie Shackleford, who at one time also used to run the Cubs. A school teacher by profession, she lived at Walnut Tree Cottage [see 4.14] before moving to Hincaster. She died in 1986.

The girls are:
Back row, left to right - Christine Thornborrow, Ruth Newby, Eileen Tomlinson, Anne Steele, Undine Miller, Gillian Lee

Front row, left to right - Brenda Robinson, Kathleen Hayton, Miss Shackleford, Violet Newby, Kathleen Wood
Seated cross legged in front – Sonia Booth

8.18 Inauguration of the new Women's Institute Bench in 1968

This picture, taken on the evening of 20 August 1968, celebrates the installation of a steel bench next to the site of the former Womens' Institute hut on Brigsteer Road [see 6.6]. The bench was donated to the parish council by the Levens branch of the W.I. to commemorate the Golden Jubilee of both the branch and the Westmorland county W.I. federation. It was constructed by the village blacksmith Joe Fletcher and installed by Alan Wilson. The presentation was made by Mrs Hilda Gladstone, president of Levens W.I., who is seated on the bench alongside Mr G.A. Martin (nearest to the camera), the chairman of Levens Parish Council. Perched on her right is Mr Norman Mason, representing the then South Westmorland Rural District Council.

Most of the other participants are known and are named in Appendix 1.

8.19 Levens Women's Institute Golden Jubilee 1967

Levens W.I. celebrated its Golden Jubilee on Saturday 23 September 1967 at 2.30pm. The event, captured in this photograph, was held at Greengate House [see 4.1] by kind invitation of Mrs Ellison. Members gathered in the garden for this group photograph to mark the occasion. Copies of this could later be obtained for the sum of 2s 6d. Witherslack W.I. presented Levens with a vase, which is still in regular use today. Mrs Ellison was given some Golden Jubilee roses.

A nearly full list of those present is shown in Appendix 3.

8.20. The Bennett Family outside Ninezergh around 1905

The farmstead of Ninezergh lies to the south west of Levens Hall. It is thought that the picture shows William Dixon Bennett and his wife Elizabeth, together with their eldest son William on the horse, outside the farmhouse at Ninezergh [see 8.12, 11.7]. The identities of the other persons are unknown (Alfred and George were their other sons). The Bennetts were at Ninezergh in the 1891 to 1911 censuses. Note that the men are all wearing wooden clogs but the boy, William, on the horse is wearing long leather riding boots, suggesting that he was not employed in heavy labour. William appears to be the recipient of a long hard stare from the severely dressed Mrs Bennett wielding a sweeping brush. Ninezergh had a reputation for being a 'hungry farm' at which the living yielded little food and hired workers would quickly move on when they had served their time.

8.21 The Bennet family of Ninezergh with working horses

This picture appears to show the same Bennet family at Ninezergh as in 8.20, but at a slightly earlier date, judging from the relative heights of the younger boys. Note the more formal dress of the people, including clean boots and a pocket watch, suggesting that they are about to take their horses to an agricultural show? At this time horses were the prime motive power on the farm. Garnett, in his book *Westmorland Agriculture 1800 – 1900* (Titus Wilson, Kendal 1912), wrote that Shire horses *'have come to the front in the Southern part of the county'*. William Cottam of nearby Nether Levens was at this time, around 1909, a prize-winning breeder of Shires [see 11.1], whereas in the northern part of the county Clydesdales were more favoured. Garnett goes on to write that *'for many years about 1880, Robert Reich of Lord's Plain was practically the only breeder of pure Clydesdales in the southern part of the county, and it might be noted that he was using a team of bullocks for ploughing about the same time'*. Horses were still employed on farms many years later [see 11.3, 11.6] but their use declined rapidly as tractors became increasingly common from the 1930s onwards. By 1951 only 27 horses, both recreational and agricultural, were exhibited at the Westmorland County Show. We are unsure who, in our district, was the last to use horses extensively on the farm. It may have been John Casson at Gilpin Bank, Lyth, in the early to mid-1960s or the Moorhouse family at Gilpin Farm.

8.22 The carriage awaits — Levens Hall around the 1880s or early 90s

The seated 'coachman' is Robert Thompson Crawshay, future brother-in-law to Josceline Bagot (light coloured overcoat) [see 9.7]. The man in the dark coat is Charles Hamilton Aide. The dog's name is Dinah: that of the groom is unrecorded. Mr Crawshay, the husband of Mary Leslie, one of Theodosia Bagot's [see 9.7] sisters [see 8.43], was a leading member of the iron-making and coal-owning Crawshay family of Cyfarthfa works near Merthyr, South Wales. Charles Hamilton Aide was born in Paris in 1826, the son of an Armenian merchant and English mother. His father was killed in a duel in 1830 and his mother brought him up in England. He attended the University of Bonn and then served in the British army for seven years, attaining the rank of Captain. He was a prolific novelist, playwright, painter, songwriter and above all, a socialite. He illustrates the variety of connections enjoyed by the Bagots, who were most certainly more than just provincial gentry.

8.23 Levens Shooting Party around the 1920s

Nothing is known about this picture except that it seems to be in Levens Park. It appears to date from the 1920s or thereabouts, when Levens Hall was let to the Reynolds family of Lancashire cotton millers during the minority of Oliver Robin Gaskell (later Bagot), heir to the estate. The clothes look more modern than those worn by the Levens Estate game-keeper Isaac Hall [see 9.16] around 1900 and the shotguns appear to be the now universal 'hammerless' variety. The gentlemen seem unconcerned about safety, standing with their guns unbroken.

8.24 Winston Churchill at Levens Hall on 15 June 1901

On this occasion Winston Churchill addressed the assembled crowd from the steps of Levens Hall [see 1.4, 4.25]. Churchill's mother, Jenny Jerome, was the sister of Léonie Jerome who was married to Theodosia Bagot's [see 9.7] brother Jack Leslie. The event shown was a rally of the South Westmorland Branch of the Primrose League. The League was an early example of a mass party political organisation and at the time was said to number 1.5 million members. It was founded in 1883 by admirers of the late Prime Minister, Benjamin Disraeli and prominent amongst its founders was Lord Randolph Churchill, Winston's father. Its aim was to gain the support of the people for Conservative Party principles and imperialism. The League took as its emblem the primrose, which had been Disraeli's favourite flower. By 1901 Primrose League rallies and other Conservative events, overseen by Josceline Bagot [see 9.7], were frequent occasions at Levens Hall. Churchill was a relative political newcomer, having been elected as MP for Oldham in the general election of 1900. The *Westmorland Gazette* at the time complimented the organisers of the event for their foresight in securing Churchill's presence, and remarked that 'they met with a reward which outstripped even the liveliest expectations and ... that Saturday's crowd exceeded all previous experience'. Churchill spoke for about an hour almost entirely about the Boer War and the report further remarked on his demeanour and eloquence, which 'may be expected to carry him far in the game of politics'

8.25 Lord Lonsdale's visit to Levens Hall in about 1911

This picture shows Lord Lonsdale's car (centre right) outside Levens Hall. [see 1.4, 4.25]. It had a body specially made to accommodate his 6' 4'' frame plus top hat. Whether the rest of the cars are part of the fleet of 11 yellow motors he maintained at Lowther Castle is not known. His penchant for the colour yellow led him to be known as the Yellow Earl. There is little evidence that he participated actively in politics and his yellow was not that of the Primrose League. The occasion depicted is, therefore, probably of a social rather than a political nature.

Hugh Cecil Lowther became the 5th Earl of Lonsdale in February 1882 at the age of 25. Already a wayward spendthrift, his extravagance mushroomed. Lowther Castle was refurbished and its park enlarged. He poured money into horse racing, hunting and other sporting activities and was the instigator of the Lonsdale Belt boxing prize. He entertained lavishly at Lowther receiving the German Kaiser twice. He perpetuated the family tradition of extra marital adventures conducting high profile affairs with the actresses Lily Langtry and Violet Cameron. In 1886 he was fined 40 shillings at Newcastle Court for unprovoked assaults on Miss Cameron's husband. This scandal and her fears that Hugh was a bad influence on his friend the Prince of Wales so concerned Queen Victoria that Hugh was persuaded to travel from 1888-89 to Arctic Canada and Alaska, a journey and adventure for which he gained some recognition.

8.26 Sir Alan Bagot's funeral at Heversham Parish Church in 1920

This picture shows the crowd at St Peter's Parish Church, Heversham for the funeral of Alan Desmond Bagot of Levens Hall. There is a legend that a gypsy crone, who had been turned away in her hour of need, laid a curse on the House of Levens that it would not pass from father to son until the river froze at its gate and a white fawn was born to the black fallow deer in Levens Park [see 1.4, 7.10]. The prophecy proved true for over 200 years up until the winter of 1896 when the river froze, a white fawn was born and Alan Bagot, the youngest of Theodosia Bagot's [see 9.7] children came into the world. Much was made of his arrival and the Levens schoolchildren were regularly invited to celebrate his birthday and later his coming of age in the Levens Welcome [see 6.13, 6.17]. Alan Bagot subsequently inherited his baronetcy, the Hall and its estates in 1913 on the death of his father Josceline. Fate, however, in the shape of the First World War was soon to intervene. While training with the 12th (Prince of Wales' Royal) Lancers in Phoenix Park, Dublin in 1916 his horse bolted and collided with a tree, smashing Alan's thigh. Despite a resultant limp he returned to active service in France and after the 1918 armistice he continued to serve on the staff at Army General Head Quarters at Montreuil. In 1919 Sir Alan went into hospital for a further operation on his leg, then travelled to the French Riviera to recuperate. There he contracted double pneumonia, and died in January 1920 at Nice. His body was returned to Levens for burial. Sir Alan was unmarried and his title died with him. His estate passed to his uncle, Richard Bagot, and on his death, to Oliver Robin Gaskell, who in 1936 changed his surname to Bagot. Alan Bagot's grave and memorial in Heversham churchyard is maintained by the Commonwealth War Graves Commission.

8.27 Levens Hall Estate tenants at Robin Bagot's 21st birthday celebration, in 1935

This group photograph shows the Levens Hall Estate tenants outside the Hall entrance [see 1.4, 4.25]. Oliver Robin Bagot, the estate owner, is standing in the middle of the second row, behind the lady with a white hat who is sitting on a blanket. Among the tenant farming families present are Alf and Annie Martin of Lord's Plain and Walter and Mary Martin of Helsington Laithes.

8.28 The visit of Diana, Princess of Wales, to Levens Hall in 1978

The photograph shows Diana, Princess of Wales, with Mr and Mrs Hal Bagot and Mr and Mrs O.R. Bagot. Diana's visit to Levens Hall [see 4.25] took place on Thursday, 10 September 1987. The occasion was in aid of Dr Barnado's and she came in her capacity as national president of the charity. Mrs Susan Bagot of Levens Hall was president of Dr Barnado's, Cumbria. Princess Diana arrived by car at 12.30 pm and local school children lined the drive. After a private luncheon, she held a reception for invited guests and then she was introduced to the young people from the Barnado's Home at Barrows Green. At 2 pm she walked around the gardens and met the invited public. The entertainment included the Phoenix Dancers, the Kendal Madrigal Singers, a Punch and Judy show, tents showcasing local crafts and the Westmorland Step and Garland Dancers. Afternoon tea was served to guests in a marquee on the lawns. The Princess departed by helicopter from the car park at 3pm. The afternoon finished with the sounding of the retreat in front of the Hall by the Band and Bugles of the Light Infantry. The weather remained fine during the visit even though in Kendal it had rained heavily.

8.29 George Formby at Levens Hall in 1938

These pictures show the well-known entertainer George Formby attending a Conservative Party Fete and Rally at Levens Hall [see 4.25]. The main party comprises of, from left to right, the Area Secretary, Mrs Robin Bagot, George Formby, Lady Maureen Stanley, Mrs George Formby, the Right Honourable Oliver Stanley, Robin Bagot and Formby's manager and his wife. Lurking in the doorway behind is 'Tarviss' the High Sherrif's butler. It is a sign of the times that only the important people were named — the others were listed by their function.

Chapter 9. Rich and poor – some local characters, worthies and luminaries

9.1 Mr and Mrs John Michie

John Michie, the son of David Michie a gamekeeper at Levens Hall, attended Levens Boys' School [see 6.4] in the early 1860s at a time when George Stabler [see 9.2] was headmaster. John Michie was to become the King's Head Forester and later the King's Factor on the Balmoral Estate on Royal Deeside. He retained a lasting friendship with his old schoolmaster, who by then was a noted amateur botanist. The two spent many a happy day wandering the hills of Deeside collecting mosses and liverworts. The results of their endeavours were published as a scientific paper entitled 'On the Hepaticae of Balmoral, Aberdeenshire' published in the *Transactions and Proceedings of the Botanical Society of Edinburgh* 22, 249-254 (1902). The Michie and Stabler families sent each other gifts of local produce, with Levens' plums finding their way to Michie's home at Danzig Shiel on the Balmoral Estate and the Stablers receiving gifts of the Queen's salmon and venison. John Michie was presented with a Faithful Service Medal by Queen Victoria in 1901 and was one of the pall bearers at her funeral. He was subsequently awarded Membership of the Royal Victorian Order in the King's Birthday Honours List for 1903.

9.2 George Stabler (1839-1910) Levens schoolmaster and botanist

George Stabler was born at Crayke, North Yorkshire. He attended school in Welburn where he came into contact with Richard Spruce, who was to become an eminent Victorian botanist. It was Spruce who mentored Stabler and encouraged his initial interest in botany. They were to become lifelong friends and correspondents on botanical matters and Stabler was the first named beneficiary in Spruce's will. George Stabler won a Queen's Scholarship to St John's College, York to train as a teacher. He was appointed schoolmaster at Levens Boys' School [see 6.4] in 1860 where he worked at the same post until ill health, in the form of partial blindness, forced his retirement in 1899. He was a respected and well-liked headmaster who struggled to provide a good education for the boys of what then was a poor rural parish with conflicting demands on his pupils' time, such as the labour requirements for harvest and peat cutting. George Stabler was a good all-round naturalist but his most significant contribution was towards our knowledge of mosses and liverworts. In particular, he published a series of nine important papers in *The Naturalist* journal between 1888 and 1898 entitled 'On the Hepaticae and Musci of Westmorland'. His name is celebrated in the plant species that were named after him, such as Stabler's Rustwort, *Marsupella stableri*. A full account of the life of George Stabler can be found in the book by Ian Hodkinson and Allan Steward (2012), *The Three-Legged Society*, Lancaster University, Centre for North-West Regional Studies.

9.3 Harold Stabler, one of the founders of Poole Pottery

Harold Stabler and his wife Phoebe, whom he married in 1906, were joint founders of Poole Pottery and are widely recognised as leading players in the Arts and Crafts Movement. Harold, the son of George Stabler [see 9.2] was born in Levens in 1872 and attended his father's school. On leaving school he was apprenticed to Arthur Simpson, the Kendal wood turner, and trained in stone and wood carving at Kendal School of Art. He left to become the first permanent Director of Keswick School of Industrial Art in 1898, a move facilitated by Edith Rawnsley, wife of Canon Rawnsley, a founder of the National Trust. In early 1900 he joined Richard Rathbone at the metalwork department of the Liverpool School of Art, where he met his wife, already a noted ceramic modeller. He followed Rathbone to London around 1902, later becoming head of the Department of Arts and Crafts at the John Cass Technical Institute, London (1907-1937) and the Royal College of Art (1912-1926). In 1921, Harold established a subsidiary company called *Carter, Stabler & Adams* for which Phoebe acted as a designer. CSA became highly successful in the production of ornamental and domestic pottery, later becoming the *Poole Pottery*. Harold never lost his link with Westmorland. In April 1909 he and Phoebe supported an exhibition and competition at Levens School that displayed their own work. Harold and Phoebe's output is now highly collectable. They are represented in most major art galleries and museums in the UK, especially the Victoria and Albert Museum A more complete account of Harold Stabler's life can be found on the Levens History Group website at:
http://www.levenshistory.co.uk/people.htm#stabler

9.4 Bertha Stabler with her pet raven outside South View in the early 1900s

Bertha Elizabeth Stabler, born 1878, was the only daughter of the Levens schoolmaster George Stabler [see 9.2]. She never married and for most of her short life (she died aged 38) she supported her father. Bertha initially provided teaching assistance in the school and later, following George's retirement through ill health, she appears to have stayed in the family home to support him. She was for many years the organist at Levens church and like her father was a keen student of the natural world, with a particular interest in wild flowers and birds. She is known to have kept at various times wild birds as pets, including the raven pictured here, as well as an owl and a magpie. Her obituary appeared in the *Westmorland Gazette* for February 1917.

9.5 Oswald Stabler around 1940

This picture shows Oswald Stabler (right), youngest son of George Stabler [see 9.2]. The woman next to him is Phyllis, the only child of Oswald's brother Edgar, who had a pharmaceutical chemist's shop in Manchester. Standing on the far left is Annie Chadwick, the seated child is Daisy Chadwick but the identity of the other seated woman is unknown. Those alive today remember Oswald as a man of increasing eccentricity, expressed in his peculiar apparel, ungainly gait and the cluttered and unkempt state of his home. He sometimes wore a sack over his shoulders instead of a coat. He frequently sported a large dark overcoat, with binder twine as a belt, and often with no trousers. One lady recalls a 'funny old man' who frightened her as a little girl. On reflection other qualities emerge, including a passionate interest in birds and natural history, his entertaining imitations of birdsong, his drawings of birds and his catching mice for the family cats. He was also reputedly a good pianist and singer. Village tradition holds that Oswald returned mentally scarred from the 1914-18 War and became a recluse. He was undoubtedly intelligent, attending Heversham Grammar School where he was commended for his work. From 1899 – 1915 his occupation was variously given as District Council Surveyor for South Westmorland District Council, Highways Superintendent and Sanitary Inspector, Land Agent, Surveyor and student, and Estate Agent.

9.6 Mary Howard of Levens Hall (1785-1877)

This portrait of Mary is by John Partridge, a portrait painter to Queen Victoria, who exhibited at the Royal Academy. From her mother, Mary inherited the estates of Castle Rising in Norfolk, Elford in Staffordshire and Ashstead Park in Surrey as well as Levens. She divided her time between these places, usually spending July to October at Levens. She was a wealthy woman and used her wealth to improve the lot of the inhabitants on her estates. She built and endowed Levens Church, provided a vicarage and started a school in the village [see 5.5, 5.7, 6.3, 6.4]. She also built the Orphans' Home in Kendal. Likewise, she greatly improved the house and gardens at Levens, adding the Howard Tower to the south wing. Her gardener, Alexander Forbes, a Scotsman from Inverness, reputedly replanted nine miles of box hedges.

The seat of her ancestors, the Earls of Suffolk, is at Charlton Park in Wiltshire. In the church there, where James Grahme is buried, is a small window dedicated to her memory. This was in recognition of her contribution to the renovation of the church.

Upon the death of Mary Howard, her Levens property passed to her nephew by marriage, General Arthur Upton. He died in 1883 and it then passed to her father's great-great nephew Josceline Bagot who was the great-great grandfather of the present occupant, Richard Bagot.

9.7 Theodosia Bagot and her first husband Josceline

Throughout her life Theodosia Bagot of Levens Hall supported several projects concerned with the war-time suffering of soldiers abroad [see 9.8]. Widowed in 1913, she had been active with her husband in raising funds for the Westmorland branch of the Royal Patriotic Fund, a charity established during the Crimean War. During the Boer War Theodosia raised funds for the Portland Hospital, named after her uncle the Duke of Portland, who subscribed £5,000 of the £12,000 needed to equip the facility. This hospital, equipped and staffed to cater for around 100 casualties, was deployed to Rondebosch and then Bloemfontein. Theodosia's role was to manage and organise supplies etc., while others did the nursing. In 1900 Lord Roberts wrote to the Duke of Portland enthusing that '...*the Portland Hospital is all that could be desired*'. Theodosia was in South Africa for six months, from December 1899 to May 1900. For this she received the Queen's South African Medal, and in 1902 she was awarded the Royal Red Cross medal. Later in the Balkan War of 1912 she organised a surgical unit for Serbia, and in 1914 went to the front with the Church Army hospital for the French, at Caen. Among the other decorations received by Theodosia Bagot were the Royal Red Cross of Serbia and the medal of Queen Elisabeth of Belgium. She was also appointed Dame of Grace of the Order of St John of Jerusalem. Her book, *Shadows Of The War* (1900), tells of her experiences in South Africa. She later married the Rev. Sidney Swann [see 9.14].

9.8 Unknown soldier in the Levens Bed during the 1914-1918 war

This photograph from the First World War shows part of the 'Friendship Hospital' at Adinkerke in Belgium. This voluntary hospital was organised by Theodosia Bagot [see 9.7] of Levens Hall for the Belgian Army, which in 1915 was in desperate need of help. Theodosia, who had worked dressing the wounded at Dunkirk in late 1914, raised funds to establish the transportable 'Hospital of Friendship' at Adinkerke. The hospital became the surgical section of the Hôpital d'Evacuation for the Belgian army. It was too close to the front for nurses to be allowed to work there and was eventually destroyed by German artillery. Nevertheless, Theodosia Bagot remained there for two years, before handing it over to the Belgian authorities. The bed was named 'Levens Bed' as it had been bought by subscriptions raised in the village.

9.9 Family gathering outside the entrance to Levens Hall in 1879
This shooting party comprises from left to right General Upton, Richard Bagot, Josceline Bagot [see 9.7] and one other unknown

9.10 Charlie Shaw, peat carrier, around 1905
The photo shows Charlie Shaw holding a basket of peats. He was a carrier to Kendal where he was known as 't'peat fella'. He lived at what is now the Gilpin Bridge Inn. He was a grocer and proprietor of the Bridge Inn. His daughter, Hannah, who worked with him, married William Withers. His father farmed at Sampool Plain which was on the site of the present Bridle Croft [see 3.12].

9.11 James Martindale Barnes (1814-1890) botanist and gentleman

James Martindal Barnes was a prominent Levens resident who became well known as a botanical authority on ferns and mosses, species of which abounded in the wet mossland areas and limestone fells around Levens. He edited the second edition of a book on Lake District ferns entitled *The Ferns of the English Lake Country with Tables of Varieties,* and Barnes's Thread Moss (*Gemmabryum barnesii*) was named after him. He lived with his family at Greengate House [see 4.1] where, in his extensive garden, he maintained his important fern collection and where he carried out his botanical experiments. The old garden area at Greengate House is now subsumed beneath a recent housing development [see 7.3-7.6]. In its heyday it attracted fern experts from all over Britain.

Barnes was born into a farming family at Kitcragg Farm Selside. As a young man he worked in commerce in Liverpool before becoming a customs officer in London. While in London, in 1845, he married Elizabeth Read. She came with a considerable dowry that allowed James to purchase Greengate House, where the couple set up home. James never felt the necessity to work again. Elizabeth died in 1859 and James then married his housekeeper and servant Mary Ann Crosby, and it was she that bore his four children. James was a keen Wesleyan Methodist and was instrumental in reviving Methodism within Levens and his eldest son Joseph Anthony [see 9.12] became an ordained minister. A full account of the life of James Martindale Barnes can be found in the book by Ian Hodkinson and Allan Steward (2012), *The Three-Legged Society,* Lancaster University, Centre for North-West Regional Studies.

9.12 Joseph Anthony Barnes as a young man around 1901

Born in Levens, Joseph Anthony Barnes was the elder son of James Martindale Barnes senior [see 9.11]. He initially followed his calling to become a Minister in the Methodist Church, attending the Wesleyan College at Headingly in Leeds, where he was for a while Assistant Tutor. He then took up ministries at Stafford, Lancaster, Cambridge and Newcastle before returning, disillusioned, to Levens in around 1901, when he resigned his ministry. He worked for a short while at Earnseat School, Arnside, where his brother James was headmaster, later marrying and settling in Kendal, where he made his living organising tours to Europe for Methodist ladies. Joseph was a prime mover in organising the fundraising for building the new Methodist chapel in Levens [see 5.12].

Following his return to Levens, Joseph became something of a local antiquary, writing a detailed account of the then recently discovered wooden Bronze Age trackways known as 'corduroy roads' at Rawson's Moss and Stakes Moss [see 12.4]. He also described an ancient stone implement, probably a whetstone, found in the peat near Gilpin Bridge (see *Transactions of the Cumberland and Westmorland Antiquarian and Archaeological Society,* 6, 335 (1906)).

9.13 John Henry Bethell (1859-1945): a famous son of Levens

John Bethell's story is remarkable: one of the children of the gardener at Sedgwick House, he was a pupil of George Stabler [see 9.2] at Levens Boys' School [see 6.4] in the early 1870s. He became probably Levens' most successful son, with a seat in the House of Lords and a home in Park Lane, London, W1. John was born in Cheshire, moving in 1869 to a cottage at Sedgwick House, home of William Wakefield, landowner, banker and gunpowder maker. In the early 1880s, following a move to London, John attended evening courses at King's College and a year later he fathered an illegitimate son, Henry, whom he acknowledged privately and continued to help throughout his later life. By 1891 he was an 'auctioneer'. Ten years later he was listed as a 'Land Agent and Auctioneer', working on his own account in Romford and employing three servants. He became well-established in local politics and was twice Mayor of West Ham and East Ham. He was a director of Barclay's Bank, and the Royal Exchange Assurance Company, and ran a land, property and surveyors business in the City of London where he held the office of Lieutenant of the City. He stood unsuccessfully as Liberal candidate for Parliament in 1894 and 1900 before being elected for Romford in the 1906 Liberal landslide that put Josceline Bagot [see 9.7] out of his Kendal Parliamentary seat. He remained an MP, first for Romford and then for East Ham North until 1922. He was knighted in 1906, becoming the first Baronet Bethell. A peerage followed in 1922 when he became Baron Bethell of Romford. A more complete story of his life can be found on the Levens History website at: http://www.levenshistory.co.uk/people/John%20Henry%20Bethell%20v3%20pics.pdf

9.14 The Reverend Sidney Swann - action man and Vicar of Levens

Sidney Swann was vicar at St John's, Levens for three years from 1912-1914 [see 5.6, 5.9]. Throughout much of his career as a man of the cloth his pastoral duties were often supplanted by more exciting challenges. In his early years he was an excellent rower and represented Cambridge three times in the Boat Race. Later, in 1911, he set a new record of 3h 50 min for rowing a single scull across the English Channel from Dover to Cap Gris-Nez in France. Two years previously, while vicar of Crosby Ravensworth, Swann had taken up the challenge by Sir William Hartley, the jam millionaire, to be the first to fly an aeroplane from Liverpool to Manchester. None of the competitors succeeded and in 1910 the Daily Mail offered £10,000 for the first successful flight from London to Manchester. Swann commenced building a new plane, without any real idea of what he was doing, in Crosby Ravensworth vicarage using local joiners and seamstresses to make the fabric covering. His plane managed at best a few stuttering yards of flight. On another occasion he cycled from Carlisle to Inverness in under 24h and on others he attempted the descents of the River Kent in a canoe and of Gaping Ghyll pothole on Ingleborough. Despite his heroic preoccupations, Swann was instrumental in making several important changes to Levens Church, including the installation of a set of bells and the construction of the lychgate. It was Captain Josceline Bagot, of Levens Hall, who offered Swann his living in Levens parish and Swann got on well with Theodosia, Josceline's wife [see 9.7]. The two served together in France and Belgium during the First World War. Josceline died in 1913. Swann, then Vicar of Morland, married Theodosia in 1920. This wedding of 'social unequals' set many a tongue wagging!

9.15 Postwoman Thelma Clarke in 1946

Thelma Clarke lived with her parents at the Post Office and General Stores on Main Street (above) [see also 2.1-2.5]. The photographs are taken from an article in *The Farmers Weekly* of 14 June 1946, in a section entitled 'Other People's Lives'. The article, written by Ursula Dracombe a professional photographer who lodged at Rockgate, follows Thelma through a day in her working life, starting with the arrival of the post from Kendal at 7.30 a.m. Thelma's subsequent progress by bicycle through the parish delivering mail illustrates vividly the rural way of life at the time and provides insights into a rapidly vanishing existence. The article recounts a number of Thelma's encounters along the way. These include a herd of cattle going down the road from milking and a trickle of women coming up the hill carrying large wicker baskets on their way to catch the bus to Kendal for their weekly shopping. It records meetings with a butcher's boy, farmyard ducks and a sheepdog puppy, and Thelma's admiration for the well-manicured vicarage garden [see 6.3] and the strawberry and potato plants at the Schoolhouse on Church Road [see 6.5]. At the Hare & Hounds [see 5.4] a group of women were waiting by the road for their post. Hereabouts, standpipes provided the water supply to most of the cottages, and nappies hung outside a cottage washhouse [see 6.19]. On Hutton Lane [see 2.14, 2.15] she found Mr Ormrod, with Peggy the pony drawing the milk cart from Lord's Plain Farm (lower picture). The final call was Cinderbarrow Farm where one of the Knipe boys tinkered with the tractor.

By 10.30 she was back at the shop where rationing and the business of coupons complicated work considerably. Also, according to Thelma, everyone expected to find the PO/shop open at all hours and sometimes it closed at late as 10 pm on Saturdays. PO duties included the delivery of telegrams within a three miles radius, or six on the half-day-closing days for Crosthwaite and Underbarrow Post Offices. Thelma was a resourceful, hard-working woman, and in the winter of 1945/46 she dragged the parcels round on a sledge when snow made bicycle deliveries too difficult.

9.16 Gamekeeper Isaac Hall outside his cottage around 1900

Little is known about this picture except that it shows Mr Hall, game-keeper at Levens Hall, outside the rear of his estate cottage in Levens Park [see 4.24]. The Levens Hall wage-books of this period record the employee's job but not their name. This anonymity of the servants of the Levens Estate [see also 8.29] jars with modern perceptions but tells us much about the social mores of the time. Isaac Hall, born in Castle-ton, Derbyshire, took up his position somewhere between 1881 and 1883. A *Westmorland Gazette* advertisement in the latter year records him as being available to show prospective tenants around Lawrence House Farm. He married a servant girl from Levens Hall, Jane Brockbank, in 1885 but they do not appear to have had children. By 1911 he had retired but was still living with Jane in an estate house. A *Westmorland Gazette* article of 10 June 1899 reports a coroner's inquest in 1899 into the suicide of Thomas Arkwright, Relieving Officer for Milnthorpe, found drowned in Levens Park. This article erroneously named the Levens Hall gamekeeper as 'James' Hall.

9.17 The Hoggarth Brothers around 1880

This photograph shows John Hoggarth, born 1819 in Beathwaite Green, on the left, and one of his brothers, possibly Septimus, born 1825. They are two of the seven children of George Hoggarth and Elizabeth Washington. George and Elizabeth were both born in 1785 and they spent their lives in Beathwaite Green, where George was a shoemaker, until his death in 1825. Elizabeth and her children then joined her brother, Stephen Washington, in Scarborough, Ontario. Stephen, who was born in 1786 in Beathwaite Green, took his farming skills to Canada where he became a 'saddlebag' preacher with the Wesleyan Methodists, and founded the Washington Church in Scarborough Village. The whole extended family was devout Wesleyan Methodist, and their story reflects a pattern of emigration followed by many other families from Westmorland in the 19th century.

The Hoggarth family was just one of several Beathwaite Green families who emigrated to Ontario, Canada in the 1820s and 1830s, following the Heversham Inclosure Award, which resulted in the ending of communal grazing on the village commons. Family names include Stainton, Langhorn, Mason, Addison, Bateman, Taylor and Heigh/Hey/Hee, and several emigrated as inter-married family groups. The Taylor and Heigh families sold their cottages to Mary Howard, who had the original Parsonage built on their sites [see 6.3].

9.18 Professor William John Stephens in about 1880

William John Stephens (1829-1890), was born on 16 July 1829 at Levens, the second son of Rev. William Stephens, the first incumbent of Levens, and his wife Alicia. He was educated at Heversham Grammar School and Marlborough College, and attended Queen's College, Oxford where he gained a first in classics and where between 1853-60 he was successively a fellow, lecturer and tutor. In 1856 he was appointed foundation headmaster of Sydney Grammar School in Australia. He resigned in 1866 after complaints that he disapproved of corporal punishment. He was a member of the Philosophical (Royal) Society of New South Wales, serving on the council, as honorary secretary and as editor of its *Transactions*. William was similarly a founding councillor of the Entomological Society of New South Wales and a foundation member of the Linnean Society of New South Wales, later serving as its president. He helped found the Zoological Society of New South Wales and the New South Wales branch of the Geographical Society of Australasia. He was at various times examiner in classics and English language and literature for the Board of National Education, an elective trustee of the Australian Museum and a trustee of the Free Public Library of New South Wales. In 1882 he was appointed to the new chair of natural history at the University of Sydney where he lectured in geology and physical geography. In 1884-85 he was also acting professor of classics.

Chapter 10. Fairs, fetes and fantasies
Levens folk at ease

10.1 Diana's Vengeance; Pastoral Play at Levens 7 August 1909

Levens villagers starred regularly in amateur theatricals.

This picture has written on it; 'P. Play Levens Gardens [see 7.7-7.9]. You will [k]now Edith [Cottam], on her right is Miss Procter Mrs Mawson's sister, behind Miss Procter Bertha Stabler. We will know Anne Powley, the half moon is Miss Cosima Holmes, the 2 Gents Gealts in the front is 2 Miss Duberrys the one in left hand corner is Sue Daffady, there is 2 Miss Mead Mil, a Miss Davis, the 2 musicians behind, they were at Holker on the Friday made over £40 clear at Levens nearly £30. Miss Mead Mil lent Edith her dress. Annie Easom was taken ill at Holker so had to stay at the Hall till Sat night so that – was one short- I wonder if you can make this out.'

10.2 Edith Cottam stars again

Another play starring Edith Cottam, this time at Levens Welcome [see 6.13, 6.14]. The title of the play is not known.

10.3 Levens Sunday School nativity play on 21 December 1942

The venue for this play was the Women's Institute [see 6.6], the play was entitled *The Inn of the Star*.

10.4 More outdoor theatricals in the grounds of Levens Hall around 1920

The title and year of the production is unknown but the costume is certainly from an earlier era than the photograph.

10.5 Another Levens theatrical production of uncertain provenance

A note attached to this photograph suggests that the venue was the Women's Institute [see 6.6], although the title of the production and date are uncertain. It appears to be a pantomime around 1937-38.

10.6 'Luck to Levens'

This picture is believed to be taken in the Milnthorpe Memorial Hall, then known as the Milnthorpe Public Rooms. The occasion and date are unknown but the event is possibly a celebration to mark the birth of Josceline Bagot's son, Alan Desmond Bagot in 1896, or an election rally for Josceline [see 9.7, 9.13], who was MP for Kendal 1892 -1906 & 1910 – 1913. The banner slogan is a shortened version of the toast 'Luck to Levens whilst t' Kent flows' that accompanied the consumption of strong Morocco ale as part of the Levens Radish Feast, held annually at Levens Hall [see 1.4, 4.25] during the 19th century (see Levens History website: http://www.levenshistory.co.uk/events.htm).

The first part of the Memorial Hall on Market Square was erected in 1843. The large assembly room where this event is taking place, was added behind the main building in 1880 at the cost of £1200, raised through the sale of £5 subscription shares. The main room had a sprung dance floor and also served as Milnthorpe Cinema between the 1920s and 1960s. Until the 1920s the old Bull's Head pub was attached to the west side of the building.

10.7 Garden fete celebrating the 1937 Coronation

We are unsure where this event took place but we are informed that it was a celebration for the coronation of King George V1. The picture appears to show a poor man's carriage, an MG marque pram, pulled by a team of wooden horses.

10.8 Prize giving at Levens Hall around 1925

We are unsure what the event was or who the people are but it is nevertheless an interesting picture of social life within the village at that time.

10.9 Children in fancy dress at the W.I. Garden Party in 1939

The party appears to be taking place in the vicarage garden [see 6.3].
The lower picture, featuring Snow White and the Seven Dwarfs and the
Bridal Party is a select group from the larger picture above. The sign to
the right of the upper picture is requesting support for local tradesman,
namely Charlie Fletcher, groceries provisions and ices, Ted Pooley, joiner, Bill Head, coalman and John Cottam of the Hare and Hounds [see
11.1].

The cast of the lower photograph is:

The Bride: Barbara Hodgson, **The Groom**: Nancy Steele, **The Three
Bridesmaids** (from the left): Marjorie and Dorothy Hodgson and Jane
Steele. **Snow White**: Betty Barker. **The Seven Dwarfs** are (kneeling left
to right): Sheila Berry, George Barker, Marjorie Berry. **Standing** (left to
right): Averil Prickett, Dorothy Dobson, Ella Berry, Mary Prickett.

10.10 Another Levens event of uncertain date

This appears to be in the vicarage gardens. The signs seem to indicate it may be a celebration of Empire Day or the Empire Exhibition of 1938.

10.11 Levens Rose Queen and attendants around 1920

The Rose Queen, Jennie Wrathall, is seen wearing the heavy cream satin train that was worn by Mrs Gandy senior [see 5.5] when she was presented at court. Her attendants (left to right) are, on the back row, Florence Butterfield, Gladys Mason, Mona Dunn, Marjorie Head, Mary Newall and Annie Fletcher. The seated page boys are Jim Halhead and Jack Appley. This may have been a one-off event as there is no record of an annual Rose Queen ceremony taking place in Levens.

10.12 'Tak hod' - Cumberland and Westmorland style wrestlers at Crosthwaite Show around 1914

Although these nine wrestlers, dressed for this most traditional of Cumbrian sports, are competing at Crosthwaite, they could equally have been at the annual, and extremely popular, Radish Feast that was held at Levens Hall on 12 May and which included wrestling matches. The costume consists of silk vest and slips with coloured trunks, often elaborately embroidered, and socks. A bout starts when the referee calls 'hods' when both contestants have joined hands behind each other's back as low down as possible. It ends when any part of a contestant's body—other than his feet - touch the ground. Some bouts may last just 10 seconds, some 10 minutes

The earliest reference to the Levens Hall bouts is in the Lonsdale Magazine of 1822, and the continuous local popularity of a sport which demands toughness, agility and concentration, is demonstrated by it being a component of each local agricultural show, the arrival of a new publican at inns, the 1919 Great War celebration, and even Levens Horticultural Society's annual show. Many local men appear in these over the years; Schollick, Philipson, Mason, Prickett, Scott, Bennett, Wilson, Dixon, Newby, Faulkner and others, but perhaps the two best known are Bland and Parsons. Jim Bland, who farmed at Ninezergh, is one of the five wrestling sons of the famous wrestler Gilpin Bland, and David Parsons is leading light of the Milnthorpe Academy, founded in 1911, and his nephew David, of Low Levens, at the Westmorland Show in 2012, won the 14 stones Championship. Another local winner is Sam Wilkinson of High Foulshaw.

10.13 Levens FC wins in France – Easter Weekend 1956 on the Continent – the 'envoi'.

`The *Westmorland Gazette* of 7 April 1956, published the following account: Levens AFC beat their French opponents, Marquise AFC by two goals to nil at Marquise, a small town near Boulogne, on Sunday. The scorers were T. Metcalfe, after a goalmouth scramble in the 20th minute, and H. Miller from a penalty after 55 minutes. The penalty was awarded after M. Coulton had been tripped in the penalty area. Levens and a club from Chichester, in Sussex, were the only successful British amateur teams out of a total of 34 welcomed in Ostend Town Hall on Friday, by the Burgomaster of Ostend. The Levens team faced a heavy social programme before the match. Two days were spent in Ostend, whence tours were made to Bruges, Brussels, Antwerp and Sluis (in Holland). The match was preceded by a parade in which the two teams marched behind the 100-strong town band to the ground. National Anthems of both countries were played, and the two flags unfurled on 40ft. flagposts. The Mayor of Marquise kicked off. The game was watched by more than 600 people. Before they left Marquise, the Mayor presented each member of the team with a marble ash tray and 200 yards of blue and white lace. The team returned to Levens on Tuesday'.

See Appendix 2 for names of those who travelled.

10.14 'Game on' at the playing field on Church Road on 19 April, 2004

The event pictured marks the 'Serving Tennis to Schools' scheme, backed by P.V. Dobson Jaguar [see 11.8], pledging £15,000 over three years in support of tennis in Cumbrian schools, which enabled tennis equipment to be handed over to Levens School.

The adults are from left to right - Bruce Lawson (Lawn Tennis Association Club Development Officer for Cumbria), Roger Shone (Headmaster, Levens School), Anthony Hesmondhalgh (Cumbria LTA President), Tim Collins (Westmorland and Lonsdale MP), Paul Fowler, (General Sales Manager for P.V. Dobson) and Jon Griffin (local LTA coach).

Chapter 11. Tractors, tillage and turbary
Working the land

11.1 John Cottam with mare and foal around 1920

This photograph shows John Cottam, landlord of the Hare and Hounds Inn [see 5.3, 5.4], posing with his family's prize-winning Shire horses. John was one of the nine children and step-children of William Cottam of Nether Levens. William took over the tenancy of Nether Levens [see 4.27] in 1884 and was widely known as one of the most successful agriculturists in the county, receiving several valuable trophies for the best - managed farm. He was also a successful exhibitor of Shire and Clydesdale horses. It is surprising therefore, that he committed suicide, by hanging in his own barn. John became landlord of the Hare and Hounds Inn, from where he also ran a haulage business, in 1933. After his death in 1961, his wife Margaret Jane 'old Ma' Cottam continued as licensee until 1967. John had formerly farmed at Low Levens but fell out with his landlord the Dallam Tower Estate. He then took over Lord's Plain farm for a time before becoming landlord at the Hare and Hounds. He was a twin to Adam Cottam, who served in World War I, and who also played the church organ.

11.2 Sheep washing in the River Kent

This picture shows Alf Leeming, Edward Lancaster, John Leeming and others, who kept sheep on Levens Marsh, washing sheep in the River Kent in 1896. The location is at Nether Levens [see 4.28], then farmed by William Cottam. At that time sheep with washed wool got 4p per head extra at market.

11.3 Harrowing and sowing on Lord's Plain in the Lyth Valley around 1940

This photograph shows how labour intensive farming was in the early to mid-20th century. It shows in the foreground Bill Mason hand sowing seed from a swill basket while in the background a fine pair of Shire horses is pulling a harrow over the ploughed furrows to break up the soil clods. The identity of the person driving the horses is uncertain.

11.4 Harvest on Lord's Plain in the Lyth Valley around 1940

This is Alfred Martin driving an early iron wheeled tractor with an attached binder. It is not easy to make out the crop but it is probably, judging from the coarseness of the stems, wheat or barley. The identity of the person on the binder is uncertain. It is notable that most of the arable land in the Lyth Valley is now under permanent grass that is harvested for silage rather than being ploughed to produce annual crops.

11.5 Tending sheep in snow on Lord's Plain in the 1940s

Lord's Plain in the Lyth Valley has long provided grazing for sheep. In the days before the drainage was improved sheep could be easily moved around in small boats when flooding occurred. The farmer's transport of the day seems to have been a horse and trap; today it would be the ubiquitous quadbike. We believe that Frank Halhead is on the left.

11.6 Ronnie Webb ploughing at Lawrence House Farm in 1942

This interesting photograph shows Ronnie Webb ploughing using an unbalanced team of three Shire horses, named Boxer, Jimmie and Blossom. This is a skilled occupation keeping a straight furrow using three horses, particularly as the one on the right of the team is smaller than the other two. Normally a more balanced team of two horses was used, as in 11.3.

11.7 The fire of 1915 at Ninezergh Farm

This picture shows the extensive damage to several buildings caused by a fire at Ninezergh Farm on 7 August 1915. Agricultural outbuildings were often used to store combustible materials such as hay and straw and were thus highly susceptible to fire risk. This was not the first fire at Ninezergh. The *Westmorland Gazette* reported a damaging hay fire in a barn in August 1898. The report illustrates the problems of dealing with such fires at that time. It recounts how Mrs Cottam sent a telegram to the police station in Kendal to raise the alarm. The fire brigade were initially slow to respond as they could only raise two horses to pull the fire engine, the others were helping out at Grasmere Sports. Nevertheless, they reached Ninezergh within 30 minutes of the fire being reported. Fortunately Mrs Cottam was insured. Similar fires were recorded at Lord's Plain in 1841 and Low Levens in 1863. The peatland mosses were also susceptible to fire, especially following periods of dry weather. During the mid- to late 18th century *The Westmorland Gazette* carried several reports of fires on Brigsteer, Foulshaw and Meathop mosses, including the horrific story of an elderly couple incinerated while sheltering from lightening in a peat stack at Foulshaw.

11.8 First poultry sheds at Low Sizergh Farm in the early 1930s – the origins of P.V. Dobson & Sons of Levens

Dobson's is a well-known local family business [see 10.4]. The Ivy House site in the village is the company HQ and the UK centre for their agricultural machinery and industrial plant business. A second business, Bridge End Garage at Gilpin Bridge, is the local dealership for Jaguar, Volvo, and Mazda cars. It is perhaps less well known that Dobson's began as a poultry producer in the chicken sheds at Low Sizergh Farm pictured above. The founder, Percy Victor Dobson, born in 1907, attended Levens School, leaving at the age of 14. As his business grew, production was transferred to the Ivy House site in 1935. However, a fire put this enterprise out of business. Mr Dobson turned his talents to becoming an agricultural contractor and engineer, branching out into haulage and dealing in used tractors and surplus military and Ministry of Agriculture equipment. After his sons Alan and Christopher joined the business in the 1950s, Dobson's acquired franchises for Nuffield tractors (1957) and JCB equipment (1959). Nuffield tractors never had as large share of the UK market as Ford or Ferguson and Dobson's moved to Massey Ferguson in 1967. This association with a more successful brand helped to ensure the success of the business. The car dealership at Bridge End Garage was an Austin-Rover franchise when purchased in 1978 and it has since been transformed beyond recognition. The garage occupies the site of one of the Bridge Row cottages where Winder Yapp [see 5.16] had his cycle repair shop.

11.9 Harry Lancaster senior and his sons Harry and Jimmy building a haystack around 1940

This photograph was taken at Low Sizergh Farm [see 11.8, 11.12, 11.13]. It shows the traditional means of storing hay as winter forage for live-stock. Harry senior is pegging twine onto the thatch top of the stack to keep it in place. The cut hay was left to dry in the fields then gathered in and used to construct these large stacks. Haystack construction was a skilled occupation as the stored hay had to be stacked in a way that kept it as dry and well-ventilated as possible. Note the way the stack is being thatched to shed rainwater. Badly stored hay would be subject to damp rot and the heat generated by decomposition could lead to spontaneous combustion. Lightning strike was also a major hazard. Nowadays the undried cut grass is often transported immediately from the meadows and used to produce silage, a fermentation product of higher nutritional value than hay. Harvesting for silage, which is more easily stored, can produce three or four cuts in a good year. Alternatively, dried hay is stored as large rolls covered in protective black polythene wrapping.

11.10 Combining at Ninezergh in 1962

This picture shows a Massey Harris 780, made in Kilmarnock in the 1950s, combining oats at Tony Gibson's farm at Ninezegh [see 11.7]. The driver is agricultural contractor Bill Moffat of Natland [see also 11.11]. The other people in the picture are Barry Cheeseman, in the woolly hat and standing next to him Alan Hayton. It is reputed that the Moffats bought the combine second-hand, it having caused the death of its previous owner. The oats would have been used for animal feed and a sign of the great changes in farming in the last fifty years is that no-one in the district now grows oats or any other traditional grain crop. Maize is now cultivated primarily as an animal feed. In the mid-19th century oats was grown locally as a staple crop, with the major part of the diet of the poor being oats-based haver bread and porridge. Another telling sign of agricultural change is the number of people involved in filling sacks with grain and ensuring the uninterrupted working of the mechanism.

11.11 A Vintage Tractor at Levens Hall in 1971

This photograph was taken at a Levens Hall steam gathering to celebrate the 50th birthday of the Levens Hall showman's engine *Bertha*. The Field Marshall tractor produced by Marshall, Sons & Co., Gainsborough, Lincolnshire is driven by Jack Moffat, an agricultural contractor from Natland who, with his son Bill, undertook its restoration. Bill wrote about their agricultural experiences in his book *Jack's Lad: The life of a Westmorland agricultural contractor, 1953-2000* (Helm Press, Natland, 2004). .

In production from 1945 to 1957, the Field Marshall, was designed primarily to pull things - a mechanical horse team – and was an updated version of designs going back to the early 1930s, A distinguishing feature was the large flywheel, hidden from view, on the off-side of the engine. Starting relied on hand-cranking or the use of a starter cartridge. In both methods the compression ratio of the cylinder was reduced through a de-compression valve and a holder with a smouldering saltpeter-impregnated wick was inserted into the engine through the square hole seen in the lower front bodywork. The starter cartridge was inserted via the cylindrical structure with the string tied around protruding from the side of the bodywork. The cartridge was fired by hitting the pimple with a hammer. This technology did not represent the future of the tractor. That lay with the Ferguson TE20 with its labour saving features and multi-purpose attachments.

11.12 Mr Strickland of Sizergh Castle harvesting at Low Sizergh Farm around 1940

An informed source suggests that this picture was taken around 1940, during the Second World War. The tractor driver was Mr Henry Hornyold-Strickland of Sizergh Castle and this picture may have been deliberately posed. The rear wheels and the badge detail on the radiator grille indicate that the tractor is a Ford Ferguson TE20s (Tractor England, 20 horsepower) [see also 11.10]. This 'little grey Fergie' did not start being manufactured in Britain until 1946, suggesting that the tractor was imported from the USA where it had been licensed by Harry Ferguson for manufacture by the Ford Motor Company since 1939. Other people in the photograph are Harry Lancaster, the tenant at Low Sizergh [see 11.8, 11.9, 11.13] working the binder, and his farm-worker Alan Wall clearing the sheaves away.

11.13 Ploughing competition at Low Sizergh Farm in 1954

This photograph taken in a field down Nannypie Lane near the River Kent shows a ploughing competition organised by the Farleton and District Ploughing Hedging and Walling Association. The tenant farmer at Low Sizergh [see also 11.8, 11.9, 11.12] was then Harry Lancaster. The tractor driver was Jim Lancaster, Harry's son, who at the time was aged about 14. The winner was Wilson Garnett from Ackenthwaite. Among the onlookers the two looking away on the right are Edwin Ellis (hat) and his son Brian (cap) of Lane Foot Farm, Kendal. The tall man with a beret and hands in pockets, just right of centre, is Danny Jackson, then of Derby Arms Farm, Witherslack. The two boys between Danny Jackson and Edwin Ellis are Peter and Bobby Henderson from Lane End Farm, Levens and, on the right of the tractor wheel, is George Park of Deepslack Farm, Whinfell. The wearing of berets is a reminder that military service was still compulsory for 18 to 20 year-olds.

11.14. Shorthorn cattle around 1930

The common breeds of farm livestock have changed markedly as time has passed. Here we see shorthorn cattle, belonging to the Lancaster family of Frosthwaite Farm, grazing in the grounds of the Levens Hotel [see 6.7, 6.8]. Shorthorns were the commonest cattle breed in Westmorland at the time, but since have been eclipsed by improved dairy breeds such as British Friesian, and the then unknown (British) Holstein. Shorthorns became increasingly important from the 1820s onwards and there are early records of the Garnett family of Low Sizergh Farm being amongst the first breeders, exhibiting them at the Kendal Agricultural Society Show.

11.15 Limekiln at Levens

Limekilns were a highly important feature of the historic Levens landscape. Slaked burnt limestone, produced from stone taken from local quarries, was spread onto the agricultural fields to reduce the acidity of the soil, particularly the acidic peatland soils of the Lyth Valley. This traditional flare-type limekiln, recognisable by any motorist travelling on the A590, stands prominently within a small limestone scarp just to the east of the southern entrance to the village along Lowgate. Before being split by the A590 in 1981, 'Big Pasture', where this kiln stands, was reputedly the largest field in Westmorland at 99 acres, stretching from Low Levens Farm [see 4.28] to Levens village. Early maps designate this field 'Stonelands', a name still borne by an adjacent residential cul-de-sac in Levens. This limekiln is shown on the First Edition Ordinance Survey 6 inch map of 1858 and a Dallam Tower Estates' map of 1775 shows a kiln in a similar location. From slow beginnings in the 1600s kiln building sprang up at quarries and farms in limestone areas to meet the demands of the 'agricultural revolution' and 'enclosures' from 1750 to 1880. Extensive lime-burning took place on Kendal Fell from 1820 onwards. Local kilns included ones at Heaves, Holeslack, Frosthwaite Farm, The Waste (half a mile south of Force Lane/A590 junction) and in Levens Park overlooking the western bank of the River Kent.

11.16 Muck spreading on fields at Causeway End, Levens in the early 1900s

In the days before artificial fertilizers, the fertility of the soil was maintained almost entirely by recycling the nutrients contained in agricultural waste, particularly the faeces of farm animals. This pictures show heaps of such 'muck' tipped on to a field on Lord's Plain at Causeway End [see 2.8, 2.9] before it was spread over the field surface as organic fertilizer. Night soil, containing human waste, was also spread extensively onto some fields as evidenced by the large amounts of discarded pottery and clay pipe fragments thrown into the waste, the remnants of which are seen when walking the fields. The smoke rising from the cottage chimneys in the lower picture originates almost certainly from the burning of locally sourced peat turves.

11.17 Peat cutting on the mosses in 1935

Peat was central to the Levens economy, so much so that the part of the village named Cotes [see 4.8] was so called because of the many peat cotes [see 5.11] or stores which were found there. Each year peat was cut on the mosses around Whitsun. When freshly cut, the peats were liable to break and had to be handled carefully. Drying time depended on the weather and peats were sometimes not ready until well into the winter. The pictures show the man cutting the peats horizontally from the face of the bank and the boy stacking them on to the peat barrow, ready to be wheeled away for stacking and drying. On the bottom right peats have been laid out to dry. The location is probably Foulshaw Mosses, with Whitbarrow behind.

In the eighteenth and nineteenth centuries many inhabitants of Levens rented strips of the moss for cutting peats and growing oats. These strips were known as moss ends. Most of the peat cutters owned a donkey and a cart [see 9.10] and often a pig. One of the last cutters with a peat cart was Dinah Scott who died in the 1950s. Whole families worked together cutting and stacking peat for two or three weeks. Later, dry peat was brought to store for the winter in the small stone-built peat cotes.

Chapter 12. Before the Romans came to Rye — the early history

12.1 The Levens Park ring cairn

This is one of several archaeologically important sites in Levens Park. Situated at the northern end of the Park, the remains of this ring cairn have been variously known as Kirks-head, Kirkstead and The Temple of Diana. The cairn and an adjacent plot were excavated by David Sturdy of London University between 1968-71 (*Scottish Archaeological Forum*. 4, 52-55) and by subsequent workers. There is evidence for several periods of human occupation at the site, from the late Mesolithic (probably earlier than 4000 B.C.), as evidenced by small flakes of flint, through to later small silver objects, possibly of Anglo-Scandinavian origin. The ring cairn itself appears to date from the early Bronze Age (around 1800 B.C.) and consists of a primary burial of cremated human remains in ceramic beakers. Two additional secondary burials were found dug into the primary burial mound. The fact that these are internments, one in a crouched position, implies they are of a later date than the cremations.

12.2 Excavated prehistoric cairn on Sizergh Fell

Sizergh Fell was an area of significant human activity in prehistoric times. The picture shows the site of the prehistoric cairn or burial mound first excavated by Professor T. McKenny Hughes (*Transactions of the Cumberland and Westmorland Antiquarian and Archaeological Society. 4,* 201-204 (1904)). Two further cairns have been excavated nearby. Re-examination of the finds from the original study together with further excavation of the same cairn revealed multiple use of the site through time. The remains of about thirteen bodies were found within the cairn structure, including both adults and children and the remains of a 36 week old foetus. The bodies from the lower part of the cairn date from the Neolithic Period (3790-3650 cal. B.C) whereas those from the upper part of the cairn are much later, dating from the Iron Age (760-640 cal. B.C). Collectively the cairns of Sizergh Fell have yielded a variety of ar-chaeological finds of different ages including a reworked stone axe, flakes from polished tools and a sandstone polishing tool, together with the remains of a ceramic cremation beaker.

12.3 Early Bronze Age Burnt Mound on the Sizergh Park Estate

This site was excavated by members of the Levens Local History group as part of the 'Dig in the Park' project in the summer of 2013. It comprised of a large mound of burnt stones sitting in a wet peatland area. Excavation of the mound and the underlying peat revealed the remains of a large wooden trough sitting on what appeared to be a network of tree roots. The wet acidic conditions had ensured their survival in good condition. The large accumulation of burnt and shattered stones suggests that the stones had been heated and placed in the trough to heat water within. The purpose of this is uncertain but it has been suggested that it might include cooking food or perhaps, more speculatively, represent a primitive sauna. Radio carbon dating of charcoal from the base of the trough and from the upper pile of stones indicate that it was in use from around 2456-2201 cal. B.C., corresponding to the transition period between the Late Neolithic and the Early Bronze Age.

12.4 Site of a mid-Bronze Age corduroy trackway at Rawson's Moss near Gilpin Bridge

Peat digging in 1897/98 revealed the remains of two sections of an ancient corduroy trackway at Stakes Moss and Rawson's Moss in the shadow of Whitbarrow. The trackways consist of cross timbers, mainly birch, laid side by side on three lines of supporting logs laid parallel to the direction of the road. Some of the larger timbers, up to 2 ½ ft thick, were split lengthways and laid face downwards. Pointed supporting stakes were driven vertically into the peat to prevent the supporting logs slipping sideways from under the trackway. Clearly this timber roadway served as a major means of human access across the wet peatlands. The site was originally described in 1904 by Joseph Anthony Barnes of Levens [see 9.12] in the *Transactions of the Cumberland and Westmorland Antiquarian and Archaeological Society*, 4, 207-210. More recent radiocarbon dating of the timbers suggests that they date from the mid-Bronze Age, around 1550-1250 cal B.C.

12.5 Iron Age skeletons at Charley Hill, Levens

Archaeological excavations in 2002 and 2003, before the building of the new housing development at Charley Hill opposite St John's Church, revealed a rare 'inhumation cemetery' of five graves in the grykes of the underlying limestone pavement,. The graves contained the remains of up to six Iron Age skeletons. Such Iron Age (800 BC to 100 AD) cemeteries are rare, since most inhumations of this period occur as individual finds in pits and ditches. Similar inhumation cemeteries, however, occur elsewhere in UK from the latter half of the Iron Age. Radio carbon dating of one of the individuals, where the skull, pelvis and leg bones survived, gave a date of 94 cal BC. So far, these are the only known Iron Age human remains in the UK's North West region.

The bodies appeared to be on their side, in a crouched position, with the head pointing north, typical of such burials where the body would probably have been tightly tied, often with men laid on their right side, women on their left. The presence of an additional jawbone in one of the graves suggests the bodies may have been 'excarnated' - that is exposed to the weather and birds for several months for the removal of soft tissue and organs - before burial. Such 'sack' or 'bag' burials, where often bones from different individuals were collected together, are common at other Iron Age sites. Further radio-carbon dating of the other remains would provide an indication of how long the cemetery had been in use.

FIBULA.

12.6 Site of the Romano-British Settlement on Sizergh Fell

This settlement site, situated on a sunny west-facing limestone terrace on Sizergh Fell, provides a commanding view of the Lyth Valley and a clear vista of the Central Lakeland Fells, especially the Langdale Pikes. Much of the original stonework was robbed to build and repair the surrounding drystone walls but the evidence for outline walls and enclosures can still be seen on the ground. The site was excavated by Professor T. McKenny Hughes (*Transactions of the Cumberland and Westmorland Antiquarian and Archaeological Society*, 12, 397-401(1912)) who found, within the building complex, the body of a young person buried in a contracted position, together with simple grave goods. These consisted of a bronze brooch/ fastener or fibula, a bronze ring and parts of a large blue glass bead. The site is typical of the small farm settlements of the early part of the first millennium AD.

Appendix 1

Inauguration of the new Women's Institute Bench in 1968

1.	Mrs Gloster	15.	Jim Hesmondhalgh - Walnut Tree
2.	Mona Hayton - formerly Latham - née Dunn	16.	Mrs Henderson - Lane End Farm
3.	May Knipe	17.	Eileen Knipe
4.	Mona Forsyth - née Price	18.	Hilda Gladstone - Middle Foulshaw Farm - (WI President)
5.	Mrs Alan Looker	19.	Alf Martin - Lord's Plain Farm (Levens PC Chairman)
6.	Denise Looker	20.	Kathleen Hesmondhalgh - Walnut Tree
7.	Mabel Fletcher	21.	Marjorie Dobson
8.	Lily Powley	22.	Myra Knipe - Cinderbarrow Farm
9.	Miss Wilkinson	23.	Gladys Rough
10.	Miss Knox-Thomas	24.	Margaret Wearden
11.	Charlie Gibson	25.	Mrs Birkett
12.	Norman Mason - Lawrence House Farm (South Westmorland RDC)	26.	Mrs Brennan
13.	Mrs Pickthall	27.	Mrs Sefton
14.	Margaret Hadwin - Levens Infants' schoolteacher		

Appendix 2

8.34 Levens FC wins in France — Easter Weekend 1956 on the Continent — the 'envoi'

1. Marjorie Garnett
2. May Newby
3. Cliff Woodbridge
4. Tom Metcalfe
5. Wright Mason
6. Harry Miller
7. Colin Sill — emigrated to East Africa
8. Steve Hawes
9. Bob Edgar
10. Edward Bland
11. Marco Rowlinson
12. Chris Dobson
13. Steamer Chadwick

Appendix 3

8.22 Levens Women's Institute Golden Jubilee 1967

1. Alice Barker	16. Mrs Wilkinson
2. Mrs Thompson.	17. Alice Holmes
3. Mrs Davis	18. Marjorie Gloster
4. Mrs Wilkinson	19. Jemima Dawson
5. Eileen Knipe	20. Mrs Ellison
6. Maureen Grindal	21. Margaret Wearden
7. Mabel Fletcher	22. Myra Knipe
8. Miss Knox-Thomas	23. Mrs Hesmondhalgh
9. Mrs Pickthall	24. Marjorie Dobson
10. Mrs Hadwin	25. Mrs Garnett
11. Miss Baker	26. Gladys Rough
12. Mona Price	27. Mrs Kershaw
13. Edith Cottam	28. Bessie Halhead
14. Mrs Tilbury	29. Hilda Gladstone
15. Mrs Tomlinson	30. Annie Grindal

Y